Competing in the Gray Zone

Russian Tactics and Western Responses

STACIE L. PETTYJOHN, BECCA WASSER

Prepared for the United States Army
Approved for public release; distribution unlimited

 ARROYO CENTER

For more information on this publication, visit www.rand.org/t/RR2791

Library of Congress Cataloging-in-Publication Data is available for this publication.
ISBN: 978-1-9774-0402-2

Published by the RAND Corporation, Santa Monica, Calif.
© Copyright 2019 RAND Corporation
RAND® is a registered trademark.

Support RAND
Make a tax-deductible charitable contribution at
www.rand.org/giving/contribute

www.rand.org

Preface

This report documents research and analysis conducted as part of a project entitled *Gray Zone War Games*, sponsored by the Office of the Deputy Chief of Staff, G-3/5/7, U.S. Army. The purpose of the project was to develop an interrelated series of expert input, tabletop, and computer-assisted war games to simulate "gray zone" activities, or measures short of war, to support analysis of strategic and operational threats and opportunities, to inform indications and warning processes, and to support U.S., UK, and other NATO strategies and force development plans.

This research was conducted within RAND Arroyo Center's Strategy, Doctrine, and Resources Program. RAND Arroyo Center, part of the RAND Corporation, is a federally funded research and development center sponsored by the United States Army.

RAND operates under a "Federal-Wide Assurance" (FWA00003425) and complies with the *Code of Federal Regulations for the Protection of Human Subjects Under United States Law* (45 CFR 46), also known as "the Common Rule," as well as with the implementation guidance set forth in DoD Instruction 3216.02. As applicable, this compliance includes reviews and approvals by RAND's Institutional Review Board (the Human Subjects Protection Committee) and by the U.S. Army. The views of sources utilized in this study are solely their own and do not represent the official policy or position of DoD or the U.S. Government.

Contents

Figures and Table

Figures

Table

Summary

Russia's 2014 offensives in the disputed regions of Crimea and the Donbass in Ukraine present a different challenge—an undeclared form of warfare that relied on a mixture of conventional and unconventional tools—from the one that the North Atlantic Treaty Organization (NATO) had prepared for during the Cold War. There have been many terms used to describe these unconventional Russian campaigns, including "gray zone conflict." This study was tasked with examining the "gray zone" in Europe, which is the expression we will use. We define gray zone tactics as *ambiguous* political, economic, informational, or military actions that primarily target domestic or international public opinion and are employed to advance a *revisionist* nation's interests without provoking outright war.

To better understand where there are vulnerabilities to these types of tactics and how to effectively counter them, we ran a series of war games to explore the issue of Russian gray zone aggression in Europe. These games comprised a Russian (Red) team, which was tasked with expanding its influence and undermining NATO unity, competing against a European (Green) team and a U.S. (Blue) team, which were aiming to defend their allies from Red's gray zone activities without provoking an outright war. In our games, we observed patterns of behavior from the three teams that are broadly consistent with what we have observed in the real world. This report presents the following key insights from these games and from the research effort that informed them:

- "Everyday" gray zone actions must be differentiated from more aggressive and focused gray zone actions. There are two variables, the target of the action and whether it involves outright violence or the threat of violence, that are important for understanding Russian gray zone tactics, because they imply different time horizons, objectives, and stakes. Many of the unconventional tactics that Russia uses to try to gain influence are routine, diffuse, and long-term, although others have very specific, short-term objectives. Russian gray zone tactics might also be nonviolent (e.g., propaganda and disinformation) or involve outright violence or the threat of violence (e.g., a planned coup in Montenegro).

- Based on the war games conducted to support this project, we observed that NATO and the European Union (EU) are unlikely to be able to compel Russia to stop using nonviolent Russian gray zone tactics, but they might be able to deter high-order aggression. There is much talk about "deterring" Russian gray zone aggression, but many of these discussions are based on a misunderstanding of the concept. Because Russia is already engaging in steady-state gray zone actions, NATO and the EU need to compel Russia to stop these activities, which is a much harder task than deterrence. Moreover, the characteristics of everyday gray zone tactics—they are largely nonmilitary, usually gradual, and difficult to decisively attribute—lower the stakes and make it difficult for the West to credibly threaten to punish Russia, even if the actions are conclusively traced back to Moscow. Outright Russian aggression with the aim of territorial expansion is an entirely different situation, and one that can be deterred by conventional means.

- Vulnerability to Russian gray zone tactics varies significantly across Europe. Russia's "near abroad"—defined as the countries around its border—is the most vulnerable region, followed by the Balkans. This is largely because of those countries' weak governmental institutions and historic, cultural, and linguistic ties to Russia. By contrast, the Baltic states are less susceptible to gray zone tactics because of their relatively good governance. Finally,

Western and Central Europe are least vulnerable to Russian gray zone actions.

- Civil organizations, rather than militaries, might be best positioned to counter Russian gray zone tactics. The vast majority of Russian gray zone tactics are not geared toward territorial gains, but instead are routine actions that seek to enhance Russia's influence through nonmilitary means. In short, this is primarily a social, political, and economic fight, not a military one, that is better waged by civilian agencies and nongovernmental organizations whose core competencies lay in these domains. The military plays an important but limited role in countering Russian gray zone activities by improving cyber defenses, enhancing intelligence and counterintelligence capabilities, and building partner special forces capacity.

- Our research suggests that the West is winning this competition but does not recognize it. Some seem to believe that, because the West cannot stop Russia from using everyday gray zone activities, it is therefore somehow losing, but this neglects the larger strategic situation. Russia's gray zone tactics will persist and should be countered by hardening Western societies against propaganda and attempts to undermine democracy. However, overreaction only serves Moscow's purposes. Strong civil societies and robust democratic institutions, rather than panic at "losing" or attempts to fight Russia blow-by-blow, are the West's best defenses against Russia's gray zone tactics. Russia's gray zone tactics signify its weakness, and the West's stronger political, cultural, and social systems will prevail over them if given the chance.

Acknowledgments

The authors would like to thank MG William Hix for the opportunity to examine an important question and MAJ Robert Kurtts for his guidance of the project. Our report was strengthened by reviews from Dara Massicot of the RAND Corporation and Michael Kofman of CNA, and we thank them for their helpful comments. We also thank the Latvian Ministry of Defense, Latvian President's Office, NATO Stratcom Centre of Excellence, Centre for East European Policy Studies, International Centre for Defence and Security, Estonian Ministry of Foreign Affairs, and Estonian National Security and Defence Coordination Unit for sharing with us their views of Russian gray zone tactics and European countermeasures.

At RAND, we thank our colleagues Jenny Oberholtzer, William Mackenzie, Stephanie Pezard, David Frelinger, David Shlapak, and Ben Connable for helping to develop and run the games, and Sally Sleeper and Jennifer Kavanagh for their guidance of the project. We also thank the players in the multiple games that we conducted at RAND for their participation and valuable insights.

Abbreviations

DDOS   distributed denial of service

DF   (Montenegrin) Democratic Front party

EU   European Union

FSB   Federal Security Service (Russia)

GRU   Main Directorate of the General Staff of the Russian Federation

MNA   Hungarian National Front

NATO   North Atlantic Treaty Organization

NGO   nongovernmental organization

RS   Republic of Srspka

SME   subject-matter expert

CHAPTER ONE

Introduction

In 2014, Russia's bloodless annexation of the Crimean Peninsula and its support of a separatist uprising in eastern Ukraine shattered the notion that Europe was peaceful and secure. It became clear that Russian President Vladimir Putin would use force to maintain Russia's influence in its "near abroad"—the former Soviet states except the Baltics—to undermine the North Atlantic Treaty Organization (NATO), divide Europe, and reduce U.S. dominance of the international order. Consequently, for the first time in several decades, NATO began to seriously grapple with how to deter and defeat aggression in its backyard. However, Russia's 2014 offensives seemed to present a different challenge—a covert form of warfare that relied on a mixture of conventional and unconventional tools—from the one that NATO had prepared for during the Cold War, one which the alliance was ill-prepared to counter. The Russian government did not officially acknowledge its offensives in Ukraine, which were characterized by the use of proxies, unmarked forces, disinformation, and cyberattacks, along with the use of conventional military forces. Together, these tactics were intended to create confusion and delay a response, allowing enough time for Russia to achieve its objective, thereby forcing its opponents to escalate the situation and mount an offensive to regain the lost territory. These tactics succeeded in paralyzing the Ukrainian government and multilateral European institutions during the Crimea operation, but did not achieve a commensurate level of success in eastern Ukraine because separatist operations in the Donbass (commonly defined as the Luhansk and Donetsk regions of Ukraine) were bogged down in a bloody, inconclusive conflict with the Ukranian government. Although Russian conventional forces played decisive roles in both operations, many observers have focused on the unconventional tools that Russia used to mask the true nature of its actions and to bolster their efficacy. Russia has employed similar techniques—in particular the use of cyberattacks, propaganda, proxy forces, and disinformation—to try to create strife or to influence elections in Western democracies.

There have been many terms used to describe these unconventional Russian actions, including "gray zone conflict," "hybrid warfare," "nonlinear warfare," "ambiguous warfare," "indirect action," "asymmetric," and "political warfare."[1] We are not going to delve into the debates about the coherence or utility of these various terms.[2] Rather, this study was tasked with examining the gray zone in Europe,

---

[1] Joseph L. Votel, "Statement of General Joseph L. Votel, U.S. Army Commander, United States Special Operations Command Before the House Armed Services Committee Subcommittee on Emerging Threats and Capabilities," March 18, 2015, p. 7; Van Jackson, "Tactics of Strategic Competition: Gray Zones, Redlines, and Conflicts Before War," *Naval War College Review*, Vol. 70, No. 3, Summer 2017; Mary E. Connell and Ryan Evans, *Russia's 'Ambiguous Warfare' and Implications for the U.S. Marine Corps*, Arlington, Va.: CNA, May 2015; Frank Hoffman, "The Contemporary Spectrum of Conflict: Protracted, Gray Zone, Ambiguous, and Hybrid Modes of War," in Dakota L. Wood, ed., *2016 Index of Military Strength: Assessing America's Ability to Provide for the Common Defense*, Washington, D.C.: Heritage Foundation, 2015; Andrew Radin, *Hybrid Warfare in the Baltics: Threats and Potential Responses*, Santa Monica, Calif.: RAND Corporation, RR-1577-AF, 2017; Mark Galeotti, "The 'Gerasimov Doctrine' and Russian Non-Linear War," *In Moscow's Shadows*, blog post, July 6, 2014; Fletcher Schoen and Christopher Lamb, *Deception, Disinformation, and Strategic Communications: How One Interagency Group Made a Major Difference*, Washington, D.C.: Institute for National Strategic Studies, June 2012, pp. 8–9; Michael J. Mazarr, *Mastering the Gray Zone: Understanding a Changing Era of Conflict*, Carlisle, Pa.: Strategic Studies Institute and U.S. Army War College Press, December 2015.

[2] Adam Elkus, "50 Shades of Gray: Why the Gray Wars Concept Lacks Strategic Sense," *War on the Rocks*, December 15, 2015; Hal Brands, "Paradoxes of the Gray Zone," Foreign Policy Research Institute, February 5, 2016; Hoffman, 2015; Nadia Schadlow, "The Problem with Hybrid Warfare," *War on the Rocks,* April 2, 2015; Frank Hoffman, "On Not-So-New Warfare: Political Warfare vs Hybrid Threats," *War on the Rocks,* July 28, 2014; Merle Maigre, *Nothing New in Hybrid Warfare: The Estonian Experience and Recommendations for NATO*, German Marshall Fund of the United States, February 2015; Kristen Ven Bruusgaard, "Crimea and Russia's Strategic Overhaul," *Parameters*, Vol. 44, No. 3, Autumn 2014, p. 81; Mark Galeotti, "Hybrid, Ambiguous, and Non-Linear? How New Is Russia's New Way of War?" *Small Wars and Insurgencies*, Vol. 27, No. 2, 2016.

which is the expression that we will use. We define *gray zone tactics* as ambiguous political, economic, informational, or military actions that primarily target domestic or international public opinion and are employed to advance a nation's interests while still aiming to avoid retaliation, escalation, or third-party intervention.[3]

The purpose of this report is to document the findings from a study of Russian gray zone tactics that included a series of war games along with in-depth research on the topic. Both forms of analysis contributed to the insights discussed later in this chapter.[4] The remainder of the report is organized as follows. Chapter Two details the methodology employed in this study. It is followed by chapters reporting the study's main insights, which include a framework to better understand Russian gray zone tactics. Finally, there is an appendix that provides more information about the war games.

---

[3] Gregory F. Treverton, Andrew Thvedt, Alicia R. Chen, Kathy Lee, and Madeline McCue, *Addressing Hybrid Threats,* Stockholm: Swedish Defence University, European Center of Excellence for Countering Hybrid Threats, May 9, 2018, p. 10; Alexander Lanoszka, "Russian Hybrid Warfare and Extended Deterrence in Eastern Europe," *International Affairs,* Vol. 92, No. 1, 2016, pp. 178–179; Radin, 2017, p. 5; Christopher S. Chivvis, *Understanding Russian 'Hybrid Warfare' and What Can Be Done About It: Addendum,* testimony before the U.S. House of Representatives Armed Services Committee, Washington, D.C., March 22, 2017, p. 2.

[4] The interaction between the war games and research is discussed further in the methodology chapter.

CHAPTER TWO

Methodology

To study the dynamics of Russia's gray zone activities, we employed two methodologies in an iterative way. Our aim was to develop a framework that could be used to understand the variety of different Russian gray zone tactics in Europe and also to inform U.S. strategic planning. To develop this framework, we combined extensive historical research and a review of relevant literature (including strategic documents, interviews, and analysis by other scholars) with a series of war games intended to both inform the ongoing research and further test emerging insights.[1] The process was iterative in that we conducted both tasks simultaneously, with the research informing the games and the games informing the research. Both activities contributed equally to the final framework and key insights presented in this report.

The gaming and research efforts were integrated in several ways. We began by researching Russia's gray zone activities, but also began running open-ended and loosely structured games with expert players. These initial games helped us gain a better understanding of the nature of the competition and focused us on particular aspects of the problem that appeared most challenging to the United States and European partners. In other words, the early games were valuable in guiding our research, pointing us toward key questions—such as whether Russia's choice to employ certain types of gray zone tactics is dependent on location, timing, and context—and insights that warranted additional investigation, such as the dominant role of civilian organizations in

---

[1] We ran a matrix gray zone game three times, a semistructured gray zone game twice, and a structured gray zone game twice.

combatting Russian gray zone tactics. At times, the games pointed us toward interesting observations that we then investigated further through research, including in interviews with subject-matter experts (SMEs) and government officials in Europe. Although players occasionally made important decisions during game play, it was mostly the postgame deliberations where we collectively considered the pros and cons of various strategies, and the competition more broadly, that led us to new insights that are expounded on throughout this report. In the later stages of the research effort, semistructured and structured games also served as a platform for testing various hypotheses and insights. Again, although player moves and game outcomes were interesting, postgame discussions with players and research team members were equally important. In several cases, after testing a hypothesis in a game, we conducted additional research to refine or improve our understanding of key dynamics.[2]

The framework and insights presented in this report are a synthesis of our research and observations made during the games and postgame discussions. The report does not describe specific moves made by the players during these games or the outcomes of the games, which could be misleading, but instead focuses exclusively on the insights that emerged from our broader cycle of gaming and research.

Designing the Games

As mentioned previously, we developed and ran several types of games. The first gray zone games were matrix games that were largely freeform exercises where the players made arguments that were judged by umpires about what they could do and to what effect.[3] We then devel-

---

[2]   An example of a hypothesis we tested in one of the structured games: Russia seeks to actively halt NATO enlargement in the Balkans.

[3]   There are three types of strategy games discussed in this report: free-form games, matrix games, and structured games. Free-form games (also known as seminar-style games) have few rules or physical elements, and game outcomes are determined by expert adjudicators in an ad-hoc way. Matrix games are a specific type of argumentation-based free-form game, where the teams present reasons why they could or their adversary could not do something,

oped a semistructured game that provided the players with a menu of options, pieces, a board, and a partially specified set of adjudication rules. Finally, we constructed a fully structured game with detailed rules that guided what the players could do and the effect of their actions.[4] Our gray zone games were intended to serve as vehicles for the players to develop coherent strategies, explore the pros and cons of different decisions, and to have a robust discussion that helped them to identify which strategies are most likely to be effective in different situations and which strategies appear the most robust against a variety of possible futures.

All of our gray zone games comprised a Russian (Red) team, tasked with expanding its influence and undermining NATO unity, competing against a European (Green) team and a U.S. (Blue) team, aiming to defend their allies from Russia's gray zone activities without provoking an outright war.[5] The players in our games were RAND Corporation experts on Russian, European, and U.S. defense and intelligence policy, and they role-played the appropriate country which aligned with their expertise.

Creating these games was an iterative process that involved extensive research on the concept of the gray zone, Russia's unconventional tactics, counteractions to Russian measures, and their effectiveness (see Figure 2.1). In the course of our research, we consulted a wide variety of sources on Russia's gray zone tactics, including journal articles, think tank studies, government reports, and periodicals. We used this

---

and then an adjudicator or umpire makes a final determination based on the net quality of the argumentation for and against an action. Structured games typically represent the phenomena with physical elements (e.g., cards and blocks) and have rules that determine game outcomes. For more on these see Becca Wasser, Jenny Oberholtzer, Stacie L. Pettyjohn, and William Mackenzie, *Gaming the Gray Zone: Observations from Designing a Structured Gray Zone Strategy Game*, Santa Monica, Calif.: RAND Corporation, RR-2915-A, 2019.

[4] John Curry and Tim Price, *Matrix Games for Modern Wargaming: Developments in Professional and Educational Wargames Innovations in Wargaming*, Vol. 2, Barking, UK: Lulu Press, Inc., August 2014; Warren Wiggins, *War Game Adjudication: Adjudication Styles*, Newport, R.I.: United States Naval War College, 2014.

[5] We follow the traditional wargaming practice of calling the U.S. team the "Blue team," U.S. allies the "Green team," and the adversary—in this instance, Russia—the "Red team."

Figure 2.1
Gray Zone Game Design Process

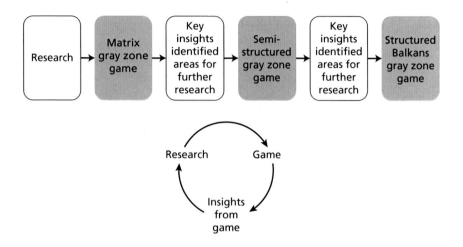

research to develop simple adjudication rule sets for the games; these rule sets distilled the existing empirical literature on individual gray zone tactics and countermeasures into a set of probability curves represented as a combat results table. These rules captured the central causal relationships of different phenomena but were simple enough that they allowed for relatively quick adjudication so that the game could be played in the course of a day. We do not claim that the rules or the underlying relationships are "correct;" rather, they are consistent with the literature and the understanding of these phenomena of the experts who played in our games, and offer a standard baseline for determining game outcomes.[6] A companion report, *Gaming the Gray Zone: Observations from Designing a Structured Gray Zone Strategy Game*, discusses the game design at greater length.

---

[6]   In the structured Balkans gray zone game, game rules were printed on cards and therefore accessible to the players, who could understand what drove outcomes. The players could then argue with the adjudicators if they believed that the rules were wrong. When the adjudicator agreed that the rules did not accurately capture a dynamic in the game, they were modified in real time and the change was noted and incorporated into future iterations of the game.

CHAPTER THREE

The Gray Zone Is More Usefully Conceptualized as a Type of Tactic, Rather Than an Operational Environment

Because there is no commonly accepted definition of the "gray zone," we began by surveying the existing literature and cataloging different definitions, and then used our early games to crystalize our own thinking about the concept. Although many conceive of the gray zone as a phase of conflict, our postgame conversations led us to recast it as a type of tactic. Identifying the *gray zone* as a tactic—rather than a type of conflict or operating environment—is a new approach, but one that has greater analytic coherence and is more useful for crafting civilian and military strategies to counter gray zone activities.

Generally, there was agreement, both among game participants and during interviews conducted as part of the broader research project, that *ambiguity* is the defining characteristic of gray zone activities.[1] There might be ambiguity about who is responsible for the actions, as was the case initially in Crimea and the Donbass; ambiguity about the legality or veracity of the claims made, as is true for much of Russia's propaganda; or ambiguity about Russia's true aims, as is true with the unstated purpose of Russia's promotion of its culture and heritage.[2] Employed in the absence of conventional war, gray zone tactics are a

---

[1] David Barno and Nora Bensahel, "Fighting and Winning in the 'Gray Zone,'" *War on the Rocks,* May 19, 2015; Brands, 2016.

[2] Christopher Paul and Miriam Matthews, *The Russian 'Firehose of Falsehood' Propaganda Model: Why It Might Work and Options to Counter It,* Santa Monica, Calif.: RAND Corporation, PE-198-OSD, 2016.

covert subset of political warfare, which was defined by George Kennan as "employment of all the means at a nation's command, short of war, to achieve its national objectives."[3] Gray zone tactics exist beyond the realm of traditional statecraft and intelligence activities, but stop short of the use of conventional military power—although as *tactics*, they might still be employed even after a conflict has escalated to the conventional level, as we have seen in Ukraine, and just as propaganda and guerrilla warfare were elements of World War II.[4]

The murky nature of gray zone tactics is often identified as critical to their success because it prevents their target from quickly recognizing the threat or from rapidly gaining support from equally undecided external actors and institutions, reducing the likelihoods of rapid retaliation or escalation. This is particularly a concern for a large multilateral organization, such as NATO, where all members of the alliance need to agree to activate the collective security clause embodied in Article V, which in turn requires them to assist the party under attack.[5] Nevertheless, the veil of deniability is often quite thin, especially when Russia has employed belligerent and militarized gray zone tactics and trained observers were able to quickly see through it as was the case of the Russian invasion of the Donbass.[6]

We focus on gray zone *tactics* versus the gray zone as a distinct type or sphere of conflict. Many others conceptualize the gray zone as a separate form of warfare that falls somewhere in the middle of a spectrum between peace and conventional war.[7] This is in line with

---

[3]   Overt political warfare or other white measures short of war are not a form of gray zone tactics. George Kennan, "George F. Kennan on Organizing Political Warfare [Redacted Version]," Wilson Center Digital Archive, April 30, 1948.

[4]   Some, such as Mazarr and Lanoszka, define gray zone tactics as something only revisionist states—those that seek to alter the status quo—use, but in fact one could argue that covert actions, which the United States and other countries employ and have used extensively in the past, are a gray zone tactic.

[5]   Mazarr, 2015, p. 39.

[6]   Andrew Roth, "From Russia, 'Tourists' Stir the Protests," *New York Times,* March 3, 2014b; Andrew Higgins, Michael R. Gordon, and Andrew Kramer, "Photos Link Masked Men in East Ukraine to Russia," *New York Times,* April 20, 2014.

[7]   Hoffman, 2015, p. 26; U.S. Special Operations Command, *The Gray Zone,* September 9, 2015, p. 1.

the U.S. military's linear phasing construct for operational plans, but has contributed to conceptual muddling because it is not clear whether there are really boundaries between the phases. At the same time, it is clear that Russia has used various forms of unconventional warfare in both peacetime and as an element of large conventional military operations.[8] The gray zone as a middling level of competition also lends support to Russia's narrative that it is not engaged in traditional aggression in such places as Georgia.[9] The conflict in the Donbass is also dominated by traditional combat with a smattering of gray zone activities that are intended to sow doubt about the true nature of the conflict.[10] It is extremely difficult to distinguish what falls in one phase versus another, and what phase a conflict is currently in, which in turn makes it difficult to identify the appropriate behavior that should follow. During their deliberations, the U.S. teams in our games struggled to determine what phase they were in at various points, and observed that the concept of the gray zone as a phase of competition was not only ambiguous and difficult to apply in practice, but also potentially inaccurate and misleading. Therefore, it is both intellectually more coherent and, for the policymaker, more operationally useful to conceptualize gray zone activities as a type of tactic rather than a unique form of conflict or operating environment.[11] Seen this way, it is clear that gray zone *tactics* might be the only or primary approach employed, or they might simply be a supplement to more-traditional warfare.

---

[8]   For more on the problems that this type of phased thinking creates for gray zone competition see: Paul Scharre, "American Strategy and the Six Phases of Grief," *War on the Rocks,* October 6, 2016.

[9]   Ariel Cohen and Robert E. Hamilton, *The Russian Military and the Georgia War: Lessons and Implications*, Carlisle: Pa.: Strategic Studies Institute, June 2011.

[10]   Michael Kofman and Matthew Rojansky, "A Closer Look at Russia's 'Hybrid War,'" *Kennan Cable,* No. 7, April 2015; Michael Kofman, "Russian Hybrid Warfare and Other Dark Arts," *War on the Rocks,* March 11, 2016; Andras Racz, *Russia's Hybrid War in Ukraine: Breaking the Enemy's Ability to Resist*, FIIA Report 43, Helsinki, Finland: Finnish Institute of International Affairs, 2015, p. 14.

[11]   This is similar to how Mazaar (2015) uses the term, p. 58. Jackson (2017) argues that it is better to look at revisionist tactics, in particular avoiding redlines, using intermediaries, and presenting a *fait accompli.*

It is also important to mention that gray zone or hybrid tactics are a Western concept and not used by Russian strategists to refer to their own actions. Writing that is often associated with Russia's hybrid strategy, such as those articles written by Russian chief of the General Staff General Valery Gerasimov, is actually describing a Western campaign of indirect action that is being waged against Russia using nonkinetic tools.[12] In the views of such authors, the West uses indirect actions to undermine unfriendly governments, which is what these authors believe happened in Ukraine.[13] This is not a radically new way of thinking about war for the Russians because the Soviet Union extensively engaged in active measures during the Cold War. Additionally, the Russian general staff has been studying asymmetry in modern conflicts for nearly 20 years.[14]

Are Gray Zone Tactics New?

Although the phrase *gray zone* is relatively new, the types of actions that it describes are not.[15] Some recently employed Russian gray zone tactics include the use of traditional and social media to spread propaganda and disinformation; cyberattacks against government communications and critical civilian infrastructure; efforts to surreptitiously buy up large stakes in key economic sectors in foreign countries or to

---

[12] See, for example, Valery Gerasimov, "Znacheniye nauki nakhoditsya v predvidenii: novyye vyzovy trebuyut pereosmysleniya form i metodov vedeniya boyevykh deystviy [The Value of Science Is in Foresight: New Challenges Demand Rethinking the Forms and Methods of Carrying Out Combat Operations]," *Voyenno-Promyshlennyy Kuryer [Military Courier]*, February 26, 2013; Vi Lutonvinov, "I ispol'zovanie nevoennykh razvitie mer dlia ukrepleniia voennoi bezopasnosti Rossiiskoi Federatsii [The Use of Nonmilitary Development Measures to Strengthen the Military Security of the Russian Federation]," *Voennaia mysl' [Military Thought]*, No. 5, May 2009; S. G. Chekinov, and S. A. Bogdanov, "Asimmetrichnyye mery po obespecheniyu voyennoy bezopasnosti Rossii [Asymmetrical Actions to Ensure Russia's Military Security]," *Voyennaya mysl' [Military Thought]*, Vol. 3, 2010.

[13] Samuel Charap, "The Ghost of Hybrid War," *Survival*, Vol. 57, No. 6, December 2015–January 2016, p. 51; Dmitry Adamsky, *Cross-Domain Coercion: The Current Russian Art of Strategy*, Proliferation Papers, No. 54, IFRI Security Studies Center, November 2015, p. 20.

[14] Herbert Romerstein, "Disinformation as a KGB Weapon in the Cold War," *Journal of Intelligence History*, Vol. 1, No. 1, 2001; and Adamsky, 2015, p. 25.

[15] Brands, 2016.

coopt business elites; support for politicians or political parties, gangs, and paramilitaries; promotion of Russian, Slavic, or Orthodox culture; and the use of unmarked soldiers or "little green men." Table 3.1 provides an overview of major types of gray zone tactics employed by Russia and examples thereof. This list is not meant to be comprehensive, but instead is intended to provide a sense of the types and breadth of Russian gray zone tactics. Russia often employs multiple combinations of gray zone tactics together.

What has been new and surprising to the United States and its European allies is the idea that they are facing a Russia that is actively and aggressively trying to influence their domestic politics and weaken the Western institutions that have underpinned the post–Cold War international order through the employment of these tactics. NATO's newest members, especially the former members of the Soviet Union and Warsaw Pact (in addition to aspirant states) are thought to be likely targets and particularly vulnerable to Russian gray zone aggression. Despite this fact, many policymakers in Europe and especially in new member states believe that accession to NATO insulates them from violent gray zone tactics. Yet, the Red teams specifically chose new and aspirant NATO members to target in our games.[16] Recently, it has also become clear that Russia has sought to interfere, albeit in a much less overt way, in the politics of longstanding NATO members.[17] In response, NATO and the European Union (EU) have focused more attention and resources on challenging Russia's unconventional tactics and have taken several steps to counter this threat.

---

[16] Montenegro, in particular, was a consistent focus for the Russia teams in our games given its recent accession to NATO.

[17] United States Senate Committee on Foreign Relations, *Putin's Asymmetric Assault on Democracy in Russia and Europe: Implications for U.S. National Security*, minority staff report, Washington, D.C.: U.S. Government Publishing Office, January 10, 2018; Matt Burgess, "Here's the First Evidence Russia Used Twitter to Influence Brexit," *Wired*, November 10, 2017; Andy Greenberg, "The NSA Confirms It: Russia Hacked French Election 'Infrastructure,'" *Wired,* May 9, 2017; Peter W. Singer, "What We Didn't Learn from Twitter's News Dump on Russiagate," *Defense One*, January 20, 2018.

Table 3.1
Russian Gray Zone Tactics

Gray Zone Tactics	Example
Religious and cultural influence	
• Promotion of Russian language and culture	• Establishment of Russian Centers in European states with ethnic Russian populations, funded by the Russkiy Mir Foundation[a]
• Expansion of Russian Orthodox Church	• The Kremlin financed the building of a Russian Orthodox Cathedral in Paris[b]
• Use Russian Orthodox Church to intervene in political issues	• The head of the Montenegrin Orthodox Church denounced Montenegro's decision to support the EU stance on Crimea[c]
• Passportization	• Intentional distribution of passports to ethnic Russians by Russian authorities in specific parts of foreign countries (e.g., Ukraine and Georgia)[d]
Propaganda and information operations	
• Disseminate propaganda through state-controlled news channels	• Crafted narrative in state media outlets that exaggerates impact of refugee crisis in Europe[e]
• Create local media outlets to promote pro-Russian messages	• Government-linked private Russian media conglomerates (e.g., Gazprom Media) broadcast popular channels with diverse programming (e.g., NTV Mir into the Baltics or the First Baltic Channel's local news program Latvian Time)[f]

Table 3.1—Continued

Gray Zone Tactics	Example
• False news and disinformation campaign	• Russian media report that NATO was planning to base nuclear weapons in Sweden as part of a broader campaign to discourage movement toward NATO[g]
• Amplify pro-Russian message with trolls and bots	• Russian trolls are used to spread disinformation in Ukraine online (e.g., denying that Russian forces are present)[h]
• Fund trolls and bots to take punitive actions against activists	• Disguised Internet Research Agency trolls and bots manipulate social media sites to get the accounts of Ukrainian activists suspended[i]
• Bribe or pressure journalists to influence content	• Paid Macedonian journalists to promote a common Slavic and Orthodox identity in their content[j]
Cyber operations	
• Hack sensitive or embarrassing information and provide to third parties to make public	• Macron campaign emails were hacked and given to WikiLeaks during the 2017 French presidential election[k]
• Disrupt online communications and commerce through distributed denial of service (DDOS) attacks	• Widespread DDOS attack against Estonian government, media, and financial institutions for two weeks in 2007[l]
• Boost pro-Russian narrative through malware attacks	• The Bedep Trojan Malware infected computers, forcing them to access a variety of pro-Russian content, artificially inflating the popularity of such content in searches[m]
• Disable or destroy infrastructure	• An explosion in Turkey damaged the Baku-Tbilisi-Ceyhan pipeline days before the Russian invasion of Georgia[n]

Table 3.1—Continued

Gray Zone Tactics	Example
• Disseminate destructive malware to disable governments and industries	• In June 2017, NotPetya malware hit Ukrainian financial, energy, and government institutions on the eve of a national holiday. The virus pretended to be ransomware, but this was deception because it actually aimed to delete and deny access to data and spread quickly to 64 countries[o]
Support for proxies	
• Provide financial support to nongovernmental organizations (NGOs) to further entrench ethnic and social cleavages	• Russian Ministry of Foreign Affairs has provided funding to the Latvian Human Rights Committee, which focuses on the Russian minority in Latvia[p]
• Develop and sustain ties to criminal networks to earn money, gain intelligence, and act as Russian agents	• Russian Federal Security Service (FSB) has ties to international criminal traffickers, including cigarette smugglers in Estonia; these ties allegedly led to the kidnapping of an Estonian intelligence officer who was investigating the illicit activity[q]
• Support paramilitaries and separatists	• In 2016, Russian military and intelligence helped to create the multinational Balkan Cossack Army, a militaristic pan-Slavic association, and tie it with the Night Wolves gang in Montenegro, which was later implicated in an attempted coup plot[r]
	• Russian Main Intelligence Directorate (GRU) ties with the Hungarian neo-Nazi group Hungarian National Front (MNA) dated back to 2012, and were revealed after an MNA leader murdered a policeman in 2016; the GRU participated in military style exercises with MNA[s]
• Provide financial support and publicity to political parties	• Russia funded the Euroskeptic and nationalist Alternative for Deutschland (AfD) party in Germany and provided positive coverage in Russian media before the 2017 elections[t]

Table 3.1—Continued

Gray Zone Tactics	Example
• Organize protests	• Russian diplomats reportedly worked with nationalists and the Orthodox church to help organize protests in the Greek town of Alexandroupolis against an agreement that ended the naming dispute over Macedonia[u]
Economic coercion	
• Secure controlling interest in critical economic sectors	• Russia's Sberbank purchased 40 percent of indebted Croatian food group Agrokor, becoming its largest shareholder[v]
• Disrupt energy flows or complicate access to energy supplies	• Russia raised gas prices for Ukraine by 80 percent in April 2014 because of an alleged export duty[w]
• Embargo goods under false pretenses	• Russian banned European pig meat, allegedly because of fears of African swine fever, during Maiden protests[x] • In 2006 and 2013, Russia banned Moldovan wine imports because of "sanitation concerns"[y]
Violent or military coercion	
• Unacknowledged military harassment	• Russian Su-24 fighters buzzed the USS *Porter* in February 2017, but Moscow denied that the incident occurred[z]
• Create and sustain frozen conflicts as a source of persistent instability	• Russia supported Transnistrian separatists with the 14th Russian Army in 1992 and then deployed "peacekeeping" forces, in addition to providing free gas and other subsidies to the breakaway Moldovan region[aa]
• Fuel civil war	• Russia provided arms, training, and direct military support to Ukrainian separatists fighting in eastern Ukraine during the 2014 conflict[bb]

Table 3.1—Continued

Gray Zone Tactics	Example
• Assassinate politicians, activists, journalists, and former officials opposed to Russian activities outside its borders	• A nerve agent was used to attempt to assassinate a former spy living in the UK in March 2018[cc]
• Attempt to oust uncooperative governments forcibly	• Russia backed a coup attempt to install a pro-Russian president in Montenegro to prevent NATO accession[dd]
• Intimidate or detain journalists	• Journalists in Ukraine were detained, harassed, and denied access by pro-Russian separatists in the Donbass[ee]
• Provide military cover to secession	• Russia supported a referendum on secession in Crimea that violated Ukraine's constitution and occurred under the cover of a Russian military occupation[ff]
• Creeping borders	• Russia incrementally shifts Georgia's internationally recognized border by moving the fence and FSB guards separating it from Russia in South Ossetia[gg]

[a] Russkiy Mir was established in 2007 by Vladimir Putin to promote Russian culture and language abroad. See map of Russia Centers, Russkiy Mir Foundation, "Russian Centers of the Russkiy Mir Foundation," webpage, undated.

[b] Andrew Higgins, "In Expanding Russian Influence, Faith Combines with Firepower," *New York Times*, September 13, 2016a.

[c] Francisco de Borja Lasheras, Vessela Tcherneva, and Fredrik Wesslau, *Return to Instability: How Migration and Great Power Politics Threaten the Western Balkans*, Brussels: European Council on Foreign Relations, European Council on Foreign Affairs, March 2016.

[d] Agnia Grigas, "How Soft Power Works: Russian Passportization and Compatriot Policies Paved Way for Crimean Annexation and War in Donbas," Atlantic Council, February 22, 2016.

[e] For other themes of Russian propaganda see Diana Kaljula and Ivo Juurvee, "Narratives About the Nordic-Baltic Countries Promoted by Russia," in *Russia's Footprint in the Nordic-Baltic Information Environment*, Report 2016/1027, Riga, Latvia: NATO Strategic Communications Centre of Excellence, January 2018, p. 61. An example of such an article is "Libya, Migrants & Karma: Europe's New Migration Policy Wrecks on North African Reality," *RT*, July 22, 2018.

Table 3.1—Continued

[f] Max Bergmann and Carolyn Kenney, *War By Other Means*, Washington, D.C.: Center for American Progress, June 6, 2017; Vera Zakem, Paul Saunders, Umida Hashimova, and P. Kathleen Hammerberg, *Mapping Russian Media Network: Media's Role in Russian Foreign Policy and Decision-Making*, Arlington, Va.: CNA, January 2018, p. 38; Todd C. Helmus, Elizabeth Bodine-Baron, Andrew Radin, Madeline Magnuson, Joshua Mendelsohn, William Marcellino, Andriy Bega, and Zev Winkleman, *Russian Social Media Influence: Understanding Russian Propaganda in Eastern Europe*, Santa Monica, Calif.: RAND Corporation, 2018, RR-2237-OSD, p. 12; Asymmetric Operations Working Group, *Ambiguous Threats and External Influences in the Baltic States, Phase 2: Assessing the Threat*, Ft. Meade, Md.: U.S. Army Asymmetric Warfare Group, Johns Hopkins Applied Physics Laboratory, November 2015, p. 29; Andris Spruds, Anda Rozukaine, Klavs Sedlenieks, Martins Daugulis, Diana Potjomkina, Beatrix Tolgyesi, and Ilvija Brug, *Internet Trolling as a Tool of Hybrid Warfare: The Case of Latvia*, Riga, Latvia: NATO Strategic Communications Centre of Excellence, July 2015, pp. 26–27.

[g] Martin Kragh and Sebastian Asberg, "Russia's Strategy for Influence Through Public Diplomacy and Active Measures: The Swedish Case," *Journal of Strategic Studies*, Vol. 40, Issue 6, 2017, p. 5.

[h] Robert Szwed, *Framing of the Ukraine-Russia Conflict in Online and Social Media*, Riga, Latvia: NATO Strategic Communications Centre of Excellence, January 2018, p. 66.

[i] Zakem et al., 2018, p. 38; Dave Lee, "The Tactics of a Russian Troll Farm," BBC News, February 16, 2018.

[j] Audrey Belford, Saska Cvetkovska, Biljana Sekulovska, and Stevan Dojcinovic, "Leaked Documents Show Russian, Serbian Attempts to Meddle in Macedonia," OCCRP, Spooks and Spin in the Balkans, blog post, June 4, 2017.

[k] Kim Willsher and Jon Henley, "Emmanuel Macron's Campaign Hacked on Eve of French Election," *The Guardian*, May 6, 2017.

[l] Joshua Davis, "Hackers Take Down the Most Wired Country in Europe," *Wired*, August 21, 2007.

[m] Rami Kogan, "Bedep Trojan Malware Spread by the Angler Exploit Kit Gets Political," *SpiderLabs Blog*, April 29, 2015.

[n] Joshua Kucera, "U.S. Intelligence: Russia Sabotaged BTC Pipeline Ahead of 2008 Georgia War," *EurasiaNet*, December 10, 2015. Russia has used cyberattacks at least twice to temporarily take down Ukraine's electricity distribution system. See U.S. Senate, *Putin's Asymmetric Assault on Democracy in Russia and Europe: Implications for U.S. National Security*, minority staff report for the Committee on Foreign Relations, Washington, D.C.: U.S. Government Publishing Office, January 10, 2018, p. 68.

[o] National Cyber Security Centre, UK Government Communications Headquarters, "Russian Military 'Almost Certainly' Responsible for Destructive 2017 Cyber-Attack," February 15, 2018; Alina Polyakova and Spencer Phipps Boyer, *The Future of Political Warfare: Russia, the West, and the Coming Age of Global Digital Competition*, Washington, D.C.: Brookings Institution, 2018, p. 14.

Table 3.1—Continued

p Alexandra Jolkina and Markian Ostaptschuk, "Activists or Kremlin Agents—Who Protects Russian-Speakers in the Baltics?" *Deutsche Welle*, December 9, 2015.

q U.S. Senate, 2018, p. 106.

r Jasna Vukicevic and Robert Coalson, "Russia's Friends Form New 'Cossak Army' in Balkans," Radio Free Europe/Radio Liberty, October 18, 2016.

s Edit Zgut, "Hungary's Pro-Kremlin Far Right Is a Regional Security Threat," *EU Observer*, December 23, 2016.

t U.S. Senate, 2018, p. 50; Simon Shuster, "How Russian Voters Fueled the Rise of Germany's Far-Right," *Time*, September 25, 2017.

u Kerin Hope, "Russia Meddles in Greek Town to Push Back the West," *Financial Times*, July 13, 2018.

v "Russia's Sberbank to Get 40 Pct of Croatia's Agrokor After Debt Conversion," Reuters, June 8, 2018.

w "UPDATE 3-Russia Raises Gas Prices for Ukraine by 80 Percent," Reuters, April 3, 2014.

x Hans Von Der Burchard, "EU Takes Billion-Euro Battle to Russia," *Politico*, January 5, 2018.

y Mark Baker, "Drinking Games," *Foreign Policy*, July 29, 2015.

z Ivan Watson and Sebastian Shukla, "Russian Fighter Jets 'Buzz' US Warship in Black Sea, Photos Show," CNN, February 16, 2017.

aa Thomas Goltz, "Letter from Eurasia: The Hidden Russian Hand," *Foreign Policy*, No. 92, Autumn 1993, p. 95; Robert Orttung and Christopher Walker, "Putin's Frozen Conflicts," *Foreign Policy*, February 13, 2015; Laura Mallonee, "Meet the People of a Soviet Country That Doesn't Exist," *Wired*, March 7, 2016.

bb Holcomb, 2017; "In U.N. Lawsuit, Ukraine Demands Russia End Support for Separatists," Reuters, January 17, 2017.

cc Elias Groll, "A Brief History of Attempted Russian Assassinations by Poison," *Foreign Policy*, March 9, 2018.

dd "Montenegro Begins Trial of Alleged Pro-Russian Coup Plotters," Reuters, July 19, 2017.

ee Roy Greenslade, "Journalists Covering the Ukraine Crisis Suffer Intimidation," *The Guardian*, July 23, 2014.

ff David M. Herszenhorn, "Crimea Votes to Secede from Ukraine as Russian Troops Keep Watch," *New York Times*, March 16, 2014.

gg Stephanie Joyce, "Along a Shifting Border, Georgia and Russia Maintain an Uneasy Peace," National Public Radio, March 13, 2017; Andrew Higgins, "In Russia's 'Frozen Zone,' a Creeping Border with Georgia," *New York Times*, October 23, 2016b.

CHAPTER FOUR

"Everyday" Gray Zone Actions Must Be Differentiated from More Aggressive, Focused Gray Zone Actions

Our research, games, and postgame discussions suggest some critical differences between the types of Russian gray zone tactics. An understanding of these differences is central to developing a clear framework and sense of how gray zone activities fit with other conventional military tactics. A recent U.S. Senate staff report expressed criticism of the U.S. government for not "hav[ing] a coherent, comprehensive and coordinated approach to the Kremlin's malign influence operations."[1] This is undeniably true, but it is in part because of the fact that there are important differences among Russia's gray zone activities that are often overlooked and which necessitate different types of responses. The first key insight emerging from the games and our research is that there are two central variables: the target of the action and whether it involves outright violence or the threat of violence. These variables are important for understanding Russian gray zone tactics because they imply different time horizons, objectives, and stakes. Many of the unconventional tactics that Russia uses to try to gain influence are routine, diffuse, and long-term, although others have very specific short-term objectives. Russian gray zone tactics might also be nonviolent, such as propaganda and disinformation, or involve outright violence or the threat of violence, such as the planned coup in Montenegro. Figure 4.1 shows how these two variables intersect to create four types of gray zone tactics and examples of each.

---

[1] U.S. Senate, 2018, p. 3.

Figure 4.1
Types and Examples of Gray Zone Tactics

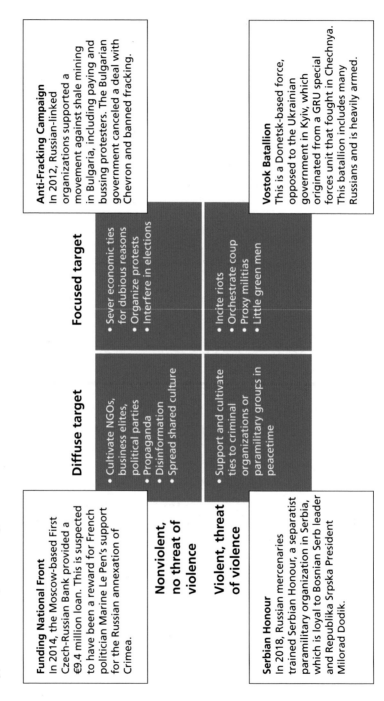

Diffuse target

Focused target

Nonviolent, no threat of violence

- Cultivate NGOs, business elites, political parties
- Propaganda
- Disinformation
- Spread shared culture

- Sever economic ties for dubious reasons
- Organize protests
- Interfere in elections

Violent, threat of violence

- Support and cultivate ties to criminal organizations or paramilitary groups in peacetime

- Incite riots
- Orchestrate coup
- Proxy militias
- Little green men

Funding National Front
In 2014, the Moscow-based First Czech-Russian Bank provided a €9.4 million loan. This is suspected to have been a reward for French politician Marine Le Pen's support for the Russian annexation of Crimea.

Serbian Honour
In 2018, Russian mercenaries trained Serbian Honour, a separatist paramilitary organization in Serbia, which is loyal to Bosnian Serb leader and Republika Srpska President Milorad Dodik.

Anti-Fracking Campaign
In 2012, Russian-linked organizations supported a movement against shale mining in Bulgaria, including paying and bussing protesters. The Bulgarian government canceled a deal with Chevron and banned fracking.

Vostok Batallion
This is a Donetsk-based force, opposed to the Ukrainian government in Kyiv, which originated from a GRU special forces unit that fought in Chechnya. This batallion includes many Russians and is heavily armed.

The upper left-hand box represents everyday nonviolent gray zone tactics, which often have very general, high-level goals, such as enhancing Russian influence, and an imprecise notion of how specific actions will create a desired effect.[2] The Russian government appears to hope that these routine gray zone actions will benefit Russia and weaken the West in some way, but exactly how, when, and why often is not known when the actions are performed.[3] The everyday gray zone activities include propaganda and disinformation disseminated through traditional media and social media outlets; efforts to promote Russian, Slavic, or Orthodox culture; cultivating allies in politics or business; gathering intelligence on government actions and key individuals; and expanding Russia's economic influence by, for example, purchasing debt or large portions of key business sectors.

Routine gray zone actions are low-cost and low-risk, which is why Russia widely and opportunistically employs them in the hope that some might ultimately pay off. Likewise, Russia also expects many of them to have little or no effect, especially in the short term. One example is the multifaceted Russian effort to promote Russian, Slavic, and Orthodox culture in its near abroad. On their face, these activities might appear benign, but they can create or deepen divisions within other countries, and provide Russia with intermediaries that it can use to further its interests, and a reason to be actively involved abroad.[4] For instance, the Federal Agency for the Commonwealth of Independent

---

[2]   U.S. Senate, *Disinformation: A Primer in Russian Active Measures and Influence Campaigns, Panel II: Hearing Before the Select Committee on Intelligence of the United States Senate*, Washington, D.C.: U.S. Government Publishing Office, March 30, 2017, pp. 1–2, testimony of Thomas Rid. According to Rid, "active measures are semi-covert or covert intelligence operations to shape an adversary's political decisions. Almost always active measures conceal or falsify the source—intelligence operators try to hind behind anonymity, or behind false flags."

[3]   Raphael S. Cohen and Andrew Radin, *Russia's Hostile Measures in Europe: Understanding the Threat*, Santa Monica, Calif.: RAND Corporation, RR-1793-A, 2019, p. 2.

[4]   Orysia Lutsevych, *Agents of the Russian World: Proxy Groups in the Contested Neighborhood*, London: Chatham House, The Royal Institute of International Affairs, April 2016; Ieva Berzina, "Russia's Compatriot Policy in the Nordic-Baltic Region," in *Russia's Footprint in the Nordic-Baltic Information Environment*, Report 2016/1027, Riga, Latvia: NATO Strategic Communications Centre of Excellence, January 2018.

States, Compatriots Living Abroad, and International Humanitarian Cooperation (commonly known as *Rossotrudnichestvo*) fosters the concept of the Russian World (*Russky Mir*) and has more than 60 centers, mainly in former Soviet states.[5] Although *Rossotrudnichestvo* is an autonomous Russian government agency, the Kremlin also supports such ostensibly independent NGOs as the World Congress of Russian Compatriots and World Without Nazism, which encourage traditional Slavic and Orthodox values and practices. These NGOs use the shared historical experience of fighting fascists during World War II as a reference point to rally opposition to current threats to traditional values, in particular Western institutions, such as the EU and NATO.[6]

Russian gray zone activities also seek to develop relationships with non-Russian partners who have similar agendas to Moscow or can indirectly advance the Kremlin's agenda. For instance, after Marine Le Pen, the president of the French National Front (now National Rally) party, publicly supported Russia's annexation of Crimea and called for the ending of economic sanctions on Russia, the Moscow-based First Czech-Russian Bank provided her party a much-needed €9.4 million loan.[7] Le Pen denied that the loan had anything to do with her stance on sanctions, although it made Le Pen a potential partner for Moscow.

The behavior and decisions of the Russia teams in our games provided some new insights and support for this framework and relationships between gray zone and more conventional activities. Specifically, these teams liberally sprinkled routine gray zone activities across as many targets as possible and then opportunistically adjusted their strategies to capitalize on previous successes. Both in our analysis of actual Russian actions and in our games, the majority of steady-state gray zone activities are long-term ventures that seek to shape public opinion, create or deepen fissures in a society, develop proxies, expand Russian media presence, and enhance Russia's ability to undertake more pointed gray zone operations in the future. Most of these measures are

---

[5] Lutsevych, 2016, p. 10.

[6] Lutsevych, 2016, pp. 12, 16.

[7] Max Seddon and Michael Stothard, "Putin Awaits Return on Le Pen Investment," *Financial Times,* May 4, 2017.

not likely to directly further Russian objectives on their own, but they might cumulatively alter the social, political, and economic fabric of a country in ways that facilitate a subtle or gradual pro-Moscow shift.

However, nonviolent gray zone tactics can also be employed in a concentrated manner to achieve a specific near-term goal, which is captured in the upper right-hand box of Figure 4.1. Examples of such behavior include organizing peaceful protests, cutting off economic exchanges for dubious reasons, and interfering in foreign elections.[8] Targeted actions often rely on mobilizing the contacts or sentiment that Russia had previously cultivated through long-term diffuse gray zone tactics. Similarly, these actions are largely reliant on opportunities and events for Russia to exploit in the target country. For example, Russia appears to have organized and resourced anti-fracking movements in Bulgaria and Romania in an effort to scuttle deals made by American energy corporations that threatened Gazprom's dominance in the region. Russia deployed a media blitz against shale exploration deals and called on a variety of old and new allies to oppose the moves, including socialist parties, the Orthodox Church, sports clubs, environmental NGOs, and business contacts. Moscow allegedly even paid to bus protestors to the demonstrations.[9]

Russia also tries to subvert the democratic processes in other countries by influencing electoral outcomes, as has been alleged in the 2016 Brexit referendum, the 2016 U.S. presidential election, and the 2017 French presidential election. Russia attempted to tilt these votes through sophisticated disinformation campaigns and cyberattacks. Although Moscow's actions might have had a significant, direct impact

---

[8] In 2014, Moscow announced a ban on Polish fruits and vegetable imports for "sanitary reasons," but it was believed to be in retaliation for EU sanctions against Russia. Polina Devitt, "Russia Bans Polish Fruit and Vegetable in Apparent Retaliation for Sanctions," *Reuters,* July 30, 2014.

[9] Andrew Higgins, "Russian Money Suspected Behind Fracking Protests," *New York Times,* November 30, 2014; Andrew MacDowall, "Chevron's Bulgaria Pull-Out a Blow for Energy Security," *Financial Times,* June 11, 2014; Sam Jones, Guy Chazan, and Christian Oliver, "NATO Claims Moscow Funding Anti-Fracking Groups," *Financial Times,* June 19, 2014; Keith Johnson, "Russia's Quiet War Against European Fracking," *Foreign Policy,* June 2014.

on the target country's policies, they still fall into the category of non-violent targeted gray zone actions because Russia acted opportunistically and exclusively used nonmilitary tools in an effort to swing the polls. In our games, Red teams always tried to sway scheduled elections because the risks of doing so were relatively low and, although the probability of obtaining a payoff was also low, the reward was potentially very high.

However, many Russian gray zone tactics have a much sharper edge than those discussed previously because they involve the threat or application of force. The lower-left hand box of Figure 4.1 shows diffuse gray zone tactics that at least implicitly involve the threat of violence, including efforts by Russia to cultivate ties to criminal or paramilitary organizations. The Kremlin and, in particular, Russia's intelligence agencies have extensive ties to the criminal underworld and use these organizations as deniable agents that can carry out such illicit tasks as strongarming opponents, gathering intelligence, and at times having individuals within these organizations act as hitmen. Additionally, criminal organizations can be used to secure cash that can fund other ventures that the Kremlin does not want to traced back to it.[10] For instance, Moscow reportedly began funding the Night Wolves motorcycle gang in 2013, and through these efforts, managed to turn the organization into an ultranationalist government proxy.[11] The Night Wolves go on tours, such as their 2018 trip to the Balkans, to propagate pro-Russian views and to impress and intimidate observers.[12]

Russia also seeks to develop relationships with paramilitary organizations. In Bosnia, for instance, the Kremlin is reportedly helping to develop Serbian Honour, a new militia loyal to Milorad Dodik, the president of the semi-autonomous Republic of Srspka (RS), who is "a

---

[10] Mark Galeotti, *Crimintern: How the Kremlin Uses Russia's Criminal Networks in Europe*, Brussels: European Council on Foreign Relations, April 2017, pp. 6–8.

[11] Mark Galeotti, "An Unusual Friendship: Bikers and the Kremlin," *Moscow Times*, July 20, 2018; Kira Harris, "Russia's Fifth Column: The Influence of the Night Wolves Motorcycle Club," *Studies in Conflict and Terrorism*, 2018.

[12] Whether the Night Wolves really intimidate has been questioned. Andrew Higgins, "Russia's Feared 'Night Wolves' Bike Gang Came to Bosnia. Bosnia Giggled," *New York Times*, March 31, 2018.

frequent visitor to Moscow."[13] Russian mercenaries with ties to the Kremlin allegedly began training Bosnian Serb recruits at a training center, funded by Moscow, in Serbia.[14] This is exacerbating already tense relations between RS and the Bosniak-Bosnian Croat Federation. RS seeks more autonomy—if not complete independence—from Bosnia, and promotes an ultranationalist Serbian agenda.[15] A Bosnian Serb paramilitary has heightened fears of sectarian violence and deepened divisions within Bosnia, and potentially could be used as a means of destabilizing the state should it seek to move closer to NATO.

Additionally, Russia has undertaken much more aggressive and directed short-term gray zone actions that involved the threat of or actual use of violence, usually when it perceived its vital interests to be at risk, which is displayed in the lower right-hand box. This category includes Russia's 2008 war in Georgia and the 2014 war in the Donbass in eastern Ukraine. From the start, the former was a conventional military offensive disguised as a peacekeeping operation, which included a small number of gray zone tactics, including cyberattacks to interrupt Georgian government communications, and a media campaign to promote the Russian government's narrative in the breakaway region of South Ossetia and to the international community.[16]

The latter operation began principally with gray zone tactics, primarily the use of Ukrainian proxies, such as the Donetsk People's Republic and Luhansk People's Republic militias, which were bolstered by both irregular and regular forces from Russia.[17] The Russian forces

---

[13] Economist Intelligence Unit, "Russia's Role in the Western Balkans," webpage, October 18, 2017.

[14] Julian Borger, "Russian-Trained Mercenaries Back Bosnia's Serb Separatists," *The Guardian*, January 12, 2018.

[15] Alan Crosby, "Here Are the Flashpoints You Should Be Watching in the Balkans," Radio Free Europe/Radio Liberty, April 28, 2017; Thomas Rosner, "The Western Balkans: A Region of Secessions," *Deutsche Welle*, October 4, 2017.

[16] Caroline V. Pallin and Fredrik Westerlund, "Russia's War in Georgia: Lessons and Consequences," *Small Wars and Insurgencies*, Vol. 20, No. 2, 2009.

[17] The Ukrainian insurgency was manufactured by the Kremlin, and the Ukrainian separatist organizations were fragmented, weak, and wholly dependent on Russian support to survive. Franklin Holcomb, *The Kremlin's Irregular Army: Ukrainian Separatist Order of*

were purported to be sympathetic "volunteers," including the Night Wolves, foreign fighters in the multinational Vostok Brigade, and Russian military personnel who supposedly took a leave of absence to support their Ukrainian allies.[18] Russia's initial strategy, which was heavily reliant on proxy and unmarked forces, failed as the Ukrainian government was able to push the separatists to the brink of defeat.[19] To save its proxies, Russia deployed large numbers of conventional forces beginning in August 2014 and moderated its goals from aiming to undermine the Ukrainian government to consolidating the separatists' foothold in the Donbass region, thereby ensuring that the conflict would continue and providing Moscow with a lever that it could use to dial up or dial down pressure on the Ukrainian government in Kyiv. Although Russian proxies and the GRU continue to be active in Ukraine, the fight is still predominantly conventional combined-arms operations of lower intensity, even though Moscow does not acknowledge its role in the war.

Even the takeover of Crimea, which arguably involved the most successful deployment of gray zone tactics to date—Russia was able to annex the peninsula without going to war—depended heavily on conventional Russian forces. While local pro-Russian self-defense "volunteers" and proxies assisted by, for example, blocking the roads in Sevastopol, the operation was led by Russian special forces (spetsnaz) and unmarked Russian soldiers from the 810th Independent Naval Infantry Brigade (a marine unit). The operation was facilitated by a large snap exercise in the Western and Central Military Districts to cover for troop movements, divert attention from the events in Crimea, and

---

Battle, Russia and Ukraine Security Report 3, Washington, D.C.: Institute for the Study of War, September 2017, p. 9.

[18] Galeotti, 2016, pp. 285–286; Racz, 2015, p. 12; Damon Tabor, "Putin's Angels: Inside Russia's Most Infamous Motorcycle Club," *Rolling Stone*, October 8, 2015; Jack Losh, "Putin's Angels: The Bikers Battling for Russia in Ukraine," *The Guardian*, January 29, 2016; Andrew Roth, "A Separatist Militia in Ukraine with Russian Fighters Holds a Key," *New York Times*, June 4, 2014a.

[19] Holcomb, 2017, p. 7.

deter the Ukrainian government from intervening.[20] In short, although gray zone tactics were employed in Georgia, Crimea, and the Donbass, all three involved Russian military forces capturing territory, and only in Crimea was conventional combat avoided.[21]

These high-intensity gray zone actions were not opportunistic, but were in reaction to a perceived threat to Russia's vital interests, specifically, the dangers posed by the potential expansion of NATO and EU membership to Georgia and Ukraine, respectively. As a result, Moscow was willing to use more risky tactics that directly involved Russian military forces and therefore had a higher probability of being uncovered and leading to unwanted consequences, as ultimately occurred in the Donbass. These Russian offensives were primarily military in nature, with support provided by diplomatic, economic, information, and cyber gray zone actions. In our games, the Russian players were quite reluctant to use military forces, even "little green men," for fear of inadvertent escalation. This result might be because the games did not present the Red teams with a scenario in which their vital interests were endangered, as they were perceived to be in 2008 and 2014. Additional iterations of the game would help to determine whether the Red teams generally preferred nonviolent gray zone tactics or whether they were willing to take covert violent action and overt military operations when the stakes were high enough, particularly when coupled with further research in this area.

There have also been less militarized—but still coercive and violent—Russian gray zone actions in response to a particular crisis, or intended to achieve a specific objective. In October 2016, Moscow conspired with two members of Montenegro's Democratic Front (DF) party and several Serb nationals to launch a last-ditch effort to derail Montenegro's entry into NATO by trying to overthrow the govern-

---

[20] Michael Kofman, Katya Migacheva, Brian Nichiporuk, Andrew Radin, Oleysa Tkacheva, and Jenny Oberholtzer, *Lessons from Russia's Operations in Crimea and Eastern Ukraine*, Santa Monica, Calif.: RAND Corporation, RR-1498-A, 2017, pp. 7–10; Galeotti, 2016, p. 285.

[21] Radin makes a similar point that so-called gray zone operations relied heavily on conventional forces. Radin, 2016, p. 7.

ment.[22] Russia only resorted to this elaborate scheme, which involved a planned attack on parliament and an assassination attempt on Montenegro's prime minister, after its softer gray zone tactics aimed at undermining Montenegrin support for NATO—including a concerted information operation campaign, funding the anti-NATO DF party, and backing anti-NATO protests—had failed.[23]

Similarly, during the 2007 "bronze soldier" incident, Russia orchestrated protests and riots in Tallinn, a siege of the Estonian embassy in Moscow, and widespread cyberattacks that disabled many Estonian websites for nearly two weeks in response to a decision by the Estonian government to relocate a Soviet World War II memorial.[24] Although the stakes were much lower in this episode, which was a test of Tallinn's resolve and Russia's ability to employ gray zone techniques, Russia was willing to use these varied gray zone tactics, including inciting violence, in an attempt to compel Tallinn to leave the bronze soldier monument in place.

---

[22] U.S. Senate, 2018, p. 77; Emily Holland and Rebecca Friedman Lissner, "Countering Russian Influence in the Balkans," *Lawfare*, August 6, 2017.

[23] Vera Zakem, Bill Rosenau, and Danielle Johnson, *Shining a Light on the Western Balkans: Internal Vulnerabilities and Malign Influence from Russia, Terrorism, and Transnational Organized Crime*, Arlington, Va.: CNA, May 2017, p. 17.

[24] U.S. Senate, 2018, p. 101.

CHAPTER FIVE

NATO and the EU Are Unlikely to Be Able to Compel Russia to Stop Using Nonviolent, Everyday Russian Gray Zone Tactics, but They Might Be Able to Deter Higher-Order Aggression

There is much talk about "deterring" Russian gray zone aggression, but many of these discussions are based on a misunderstanding of the concept. Both deterrence and compellence are types of coercive threats that work by altering a target's expectations about future pain, but deterrent threats aim to persuade the target not to initiate a particular action, and compellent threats aim to convince the target to change its behavior. As one of our players observed, because Russia is *already* engaging in diffuse gray zone actions, NATO and the EU need to *compel* Russia to stop these activities, which is a much harder task than deterrence.[1] To date, NATO and the EU remain focused on deterrence, rather than compellance, making this proposition a shift in these institutions' approach.

To successfully deter, one must credibly threaten painful consequences, which involves demonstrating a capability and willingness to follow through on that threat and waiting to see whether the target complies. In contrast, to successfully compel a target to reverse or halt its ongoing behavior, one must actually inflict pain and couple it with a promise to end the pain if the target relents. It is not clear that NATO

---

[1] Compellence requires the target to change its ongoing behavior—in which it is invested—at some cost to its reputation. To compel a target, one must alter or reduce the utility of its current course of action compared with the utility of ceasing. Thomas C. Schelling, *Arms and Influence*, New Haven, Conn.: Harvard University Press, 1966, pp. 69–90.

and the EU would go beyond the economic sanctions that are already in place to compel Russia to end its use of diffuse gray zone tactics.[2] Both the Green and Blue players in our games struggled to identify actions that they deemed to be sufficiently compellent *and* would be willing to implement. Moreover, the characteristics of routine or everyday gray zone tactics—the fact that they are largely nonmilitary, usually gradual, and difficult to decisively attribute—lowers the stakes and makes it difficult for the West to credibly threaten to punish Russia, even if the actions are conclusively traced back to Moscow.

Because many gray zone tactics are cheap in terms of cost and risk, Russia is willing to liberally use them even when the prospect of success is low. The Red teams in our games mirrored the real Russian government's indifference to having its covert gray zone activities uncovered, in part because of the lack of credible punishment. The Green and Blue players spent considerable time and effort trying to expose Red's clandestine activities, but even when they succeeded, this had little effect on any of the teams' behavior: Red teams continued their covert meddling as if nothing had happened, and the Green and Blue teams still found it hard to come up with credible ways to counter Red's activities or punish Red for engaging in them. Consequently, the Red teams saw nearly no downside to extensively making use of routine gray zone actions in the hopes that some would have an impact.

Even if more assertive and violent efforts—such as destabilizing a country or attempting to forcibly change the government through a coup—failed or were uncovered, there were few negative consequences for the Red teams in our games. This tracks not just with recent experience but also broader Cold War history. The United States was never able to halt Soviet active measures, which were the normal state of affairs during the Cold War: The Soviet Union conducted more than 10,000 individual disinformation operations during this time.[3]

Because of the challenges of attribution, deterrent threats against even targeted, nonviolent gray zone actions are not likely to be highly

---

[2]   There are already many people calling for an end to the sanctions, despite Russia's continued use of diffuse and targeted nonviolent gray zone tactics across Europe.

[3]   U.S. Senate, 2017, p. 2.

credible. It stretches the bounds of credulity to believe that a democratic country, which requires the support of its population, would take potentially costly coercive actions when the majority of its public remains unconvinced about who is responsible for a nonviolent attack. The need to convince 29 nations in the alliance makes it even less likely that a NATO threat would be viewed as credible. Although NATO has claimed that its Article V collective security clause applies to cyberattacks against members, it has not clearly articulated what types of cyberattacks would trigger this and what actions it would take in response. Establishing that Moscow is behind a gray zone tactic might put sensitive intelligence sources at risk and is also likely to take a considerable amount of time. For example, although the Federal Bureau of Investigation began to investigate Russian interference in the 2016 U.S. presidential election in June 2016, the investigation was still ongoing as of June 2019. The fact that consequences are not likely to be automatic or quickly implemented poses a further challenge to deterrence. Clandestine forms of retaliation, such as cyberattacks or covert action, might be possible because the public is not consulted, but these options are in and of themselves risky, cannot be threatened publicly, might be limited by the laws of a country, and therefore do not form the basis for a strong deterrent threat. Given these manifold challenges, it seems more effective to focus on improving the resiliency of vulnerable nations and taking other defensive measures to limit the effectiveness of Russian intervention, rather than focusing on deterring most gray zone tactics.

Outright Russian aggression—including gray zone tactics with the aim of territorial expansion—is an entirely different situation, and one that can be deterred. Because NATO did not have a security commitment or forces in place to defend Ukraine or Georgia, any attempts to deter Russia would likely have lacked credibility. In the future the alliance could, however, make it clear that it plans to stop aggression—whether conventional or masked by gray zone tactics—against any of its members. Doing so requires NATO to demonstrate the will and capability to act quickly to stop Russia from achieving its objectives, as deterrence by denial would in any situation.[4] NATO military and intelligence services need to be on alert for Russian preparations disguised as gray zone subterfuge that could signal aggressive intentions. At the same time, political leaders need to be prepared for this eventuality and ready to listen to military and intelligence assessments so that they can quickly see through any ambiguity and take the appropriate actions. Both of these steps need to be buttressed by a military posture that would lend credibility to political leaders' warnings or threats about the consequences should Russia persist.

---

[4]   Deterrence by punishment, the other alternative mode, does not appear to be a strong approach for dealing with Russian aggression against NATO. See David A. Shlapak, *The Russia Challenge*, Santa Monica, Calif.: RAND Corporation, PE-250-A, 2018; David A. Shlapak and Michael W. Johnson, *Reinforcing Deterrence on NATO's Eastern Flank: Wargaming the Defense of the Baltics*, Santa Monica, Calif.: RAND Corporation, RR-1253-A, 2016; Michael Petersen, "The Perils of Conventional Deterrence by Punishment," *War on the Rocks*, November 11, 2016.

CHAPTER SIX

Vulnerability to Russian Gray Zone Tactics Varies Significantly Across Europe

Russia employs gray zone tactics across Europe, but its interests vary, and its ability to successfully achieve its objectives through these means largely depends on the vulnerability of the targeted country.[1] This insight emerged from both our games and our analysis of past historical cases. In one of our early games, the Red team drew a map of Europe and defined different regions in which Russia had varied levels of interest and, in the Red team's perception, a different ability to influence because of the strengths and weaknesses of the countries in each area. Gray zone tactics often work best when they exacerbate preexisting tensions. Vulnerabilities fall into two different but not mutually exclusive categories: state fragility and polarization, and characteristics that provide Russia with leverage over the government and society.[2]

Fragile states provide openings because they suffer from pernicious factors, such as corruption; poverty; and political divisions, sectarian divisions, ethnic divisions, or some combination thereof, which can be exploited by Moscow's gray zone tactics to create instability.

---

[1] Treverton et al., 2018, p. 63.

[2] In the structured Balkans game, these factors affected a country's governance and orientation scores, which were relative, ordinal scales ranking from –2 to +2. Governance was a composite metric based on the Fund for Peace's Fragile States Index and the World Bank Worldwide Governance Indicators, although the orientation score was based on a more qualitative reading of the composition of a country's ethnic makeup, religious beliefs, and culture and its current attitudes toward Russia. As a part of scoring countries, we had regional experts review our initial scores and the justification for them. See Fund for Peace, "Fragile States Index," webpage, 2019; World Bank Group, "Worldwide Governance Indicators," webpage, 2019.

The politics in even relatively strong states might become polarized over divisive issues (e.g., immigration), opening avenues for Russian subversive actions. Countries can have cultural, economic, or historic ties to Russia that make it particularly susceptible to Russian gray zone influences. Proximity and, in particular, a shared border with Russia also ease Russian access to a country and concomitantly increase Russia's ability to undertake violent gray zone tactics. Economic dependence, particularly on Russian energy, is also an avenue that Moscow has been willing to exploit.

Although there are significant intraregional differences, one can identify four broad European regions—Russia's near abroad, the Baltics, the Balkans, and Western and Central Europe—where Russia's interests differ. But across these regions, there are roughly similar degrees of vulnerability to gray zone actions. This is depicted in Figure 6.1. Our games suggest that considering these four regions as distinct when preparing and planning to confront Russian gray zone tactics might be valuable, because of Russia's differing interests and the variation in vulnerabilities across these areas. The Red teams in our games emphasized that their interests varied across these areas and developed strategies unique to each region, based on their different objectives. Understanding these differences in interests, objectives, and existing vulnerabilities better enables NATO and the EU to identify the tools best used to counteract Russian gray zone tactics in different regions.

The countries that were identified of greatest importance were in Russia's near abroad: Armenia, Azerbaijan, Belarus, Georgia, and Ukraine.[3] Russia desires influence over these former Soviet states not only because of their shared history and language, but most importantly because these bordering nations provide an important defensive buffer against external attack.[4] Therefore, Russia views the expansion of NATO or the EU into its near abroad as a grave threat that must be stopped. The 2008 and 2014 Russian wars in Georgia and Ukraine

---

[3] The former Soviet republics in Central Asia are also usually included in the near abroad, but they were not a part these games.

[4] Andrew Radin and Clint Reach, *Russian Views of the International Order*, Santa Monica, Calif.: RAND Corporation, RR-1826-OSD, 2017, pp. 8–12.

**Figure 6.1
Intra-European Vulnerability to Russian Gray Zone Tactics**

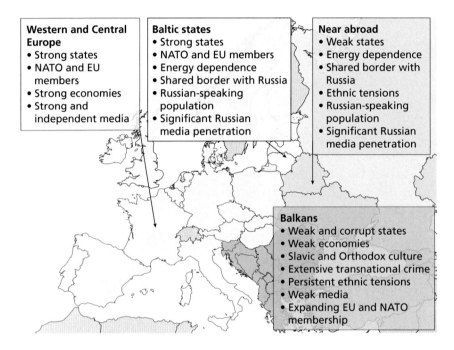

Western and Central Europe
- Strong states
- NATO and EU members
- Strong economies
- Strong and independent media

Baltic states
- Strong states
- NATO and EU members
- Energy dependence
- Shared border with Russia
- Russian-speaking population
- Significant Russian media penetration

Near abroad
- Weak states
- Energy dependence
- Shared border with Russia
- Ethnic tensions
- Russian-speaking population
- Significant Russian media penetration

Balkans
- Weak and corrupt states
- Weak economies
- Slavic and Orthodox culture
- Extensive transnational crime
- Persistent ethnic tensions
- Weak media
- Expanding EU and NATO membership

were launched to thwart their membership bids by generating a persistent source of instability that would ward off further integration with the West.

Near-abroad nations bordering Russia have relatively weak militaries and poor governance, leaving them with few defenses against a Russian conventional offensive or clandestine infiltration, including land grabs by little green men. All also contain large Russian-speaking minorities that have historical, cultural, and economic links to Russia; these populations are consumers of Russian-controlled media and are potentially sympathetic audiences for gray zone information tactics.

By contrast, the Baltic states of Estonia, Latvia, and Lithuania are also former members of the Soviet Union, are adjacent to Russia, and Estonia and Latvia have sizable Russian-speaking minorities. However, they appear to be less susceptible to gray zone tactics than some other regions.[5] This is due in part to the Baltic nations taking steps to miti-gate some of their vulnerabilities. Estonia, for instance, has invested heavily in cyber defenses since the bronze soldier crisis, and all three nations are taking steps to reduce their dependence on Russian energy imports.[6] Additionally, the Baltic nations are relatively prosperous compared with other Eastern European nations and Russia, reducing the level of economic discontent into which the Kremlin can tap. Nev-ertheless, the Russian minority in the Baltics is less well-off than the rest of the population, in large part because economic opportunities still largely depend on being able to speak the official state language (i.e., not Russian); consequently, the Russian minority potentially could become aggrieved in the future.[7] Moreover, a favorite theme of the Russian media (which is popular among the Estonian and Lat-vian Russian-speaking populations) is how the Baltic states discrimi-nate against their Russian minorities. To date, however, this message does not seem to resonate, because the benefits of living within the EU members of the Baltics—as opposed to Russia—seem to outweigh the relative disparity between Russian-speakers and the larger Estonian and Latvian populations.

The Baltics' most important defense against Russian gray zone attacks stems from the relative strength of their government institu-tions, which make them harder targets and better able to respond to covert infiltration than other former Soviet republics.[8] For instance, the Estonian defense chief stated that, if Russian special forces or clan-destine agents entered their territory, they would "shoot the first one to appear."[9] All three Baltic nations have amended their laws to enable

---

[5]   Many argue that despite the fact that the Baltics are former members of the Soviet Union, they are of lesser interest to Russia since 2003.

[6]   Damien McGuinness, "How a Cyber Attack Transformed Estonia," BBC News, April 27, 2017; Simon Hoellerbauer, "Baltic Energy Sources: Diversifying Away from Russia," Foreign Policy Research Institute, June 14, 2017; Asymmetric Operations Working Group, 2015, pp. 17–20.

[7]   Asymmetric Operations Working Group, 2015, pp. 24–28.

[8]   Asymmetric Operations Working Group, 2015, pp. 4–5.

[9]   Sam Jones, "Estonia Ready to Deal with Russia's 'Little Green Men,'" *Financial Times*, May 13, 2015.

their national militaries to operate in their countries during peacetime, and Estonia and Lithuania have exercised this capability.[10] Additionally, because the Baltics are members of NATO, and the alliance has stationed multinational battlegroups in each country, Russian covert infiltration or outright aggression is much riskier than in its near abroad.

Moreover, unlike Ukraine or Georgia, Russia does not seem to consider the Baltic states to be a critical part of its sphere of influence; instead, it aims to use the Baltics as a lever to destabilize and discredit NATO.[11] Given these factors, it appears that, although Russia could and has sought to destabilize Estonia, Latvia, and Lithuania through everyday gray zone operations, these tactics are likely to have limited effects. The Baltic states are also not particularly susceptible to clandestine land grabs. However, despite the enhanced forward posture, they remain vulnerable to a conventional offensive cloaked in gray zone tactics, especially information operations.[12]

There is considerable variation within the Balkans, but, in general, this region is an inviting target for Russian gray zone actions because of the weak rule of law, ethnic divisions, and relative poverty.[13] Nevertheless, because the Balkans are not contiguous with Russia and do not have significant Russian-speaking populations, Russia's gray zone activities would have a somewhat different character than the actions it takes in the former Soviet states, and are less likely to swing these states in a durably pro-Russian direction.

As a whole, the Balkans suffer from weak government institutions, resulting in autocratic leaders who can run roughshod over feeble

---

[10] Asymmetric Operations Working Group, 2015, p. 6.

[11] Radin and Reach, 2017, p. 10; Dmitri V. Trenin, *Post-Imperium: A Eurasian Story*, Washington, D.C.: Carnegie Endowment for International Peace, 2011, p. 107; Asymmetric Operations Working Group, 2015, p. 14.

[12] Radin, 2017, p. 31. For more on conventional vulnerability, see Shlapak and Johnson, 2016.

[13] There is no agreed definition of the Balkans. We consider the Balkans to include Albania, Bosnia and Herzegovina, Bulgaria, Croatia, Kosovo, North Macedonia, Montenegro, Romania, Serbia, and Slovenia.

civil society, a subservient media, pervasive corruption, and extensive transnational criminal organizations.[14] The Balkans are also the poorest region in Europe with high unemployment rates, which means that there is widespread dissatisfaction and resentment toward Europe as a whole, which can be exploited by Russia.[15] Finally, the Balkans remain afflicted by ethnic tensions, currently being rekindled by a renewed focus on historic grievances and another surge of nationalist sentiment in the region.[16] Ethnic violence and secessionist movements are particularly a problem in the former Yugoslavia (Bosnia and Herzegovina, Croatia, North Macedonia, Montenegro, Serbia, and Slovenia), where Russia has historic, religious, and linguistic ties to several groups.

Opinions about Russia vary significantly in different Balkan nations; in some, such as the Slavic language–speaking nations of Bulgaria and Serbia, a sizable part of the population views Russia positively.[17] But unlike the near abroad, where Russian gray zone activities primarily focus on already sympathetic populations, Russia courts allies on multiple sides in many Balkan nations. This places Moscow in a good position to stoke tensions, provoke sectarian violence, or encourage separatism. Yet because the nearest Russian military forces are stationed in Crimea, this region is less at risk for a covert territorial attack or conventional Russian aggression accompanied by gray zone activities.

In terms of Russia's interests, the Balkans are a lower priority than the near abroad, but remain an area where Moscow desires to at least maintain—if not expand—its sway and curb Western influence.[18]

---

[14] Zakem, et al., May 2017, pp. 1–2.

[15] Zakem et al., 2017, p. 6; Martin Russell, *At a Glance: Russia in the Western Balkans*, European Parliament Members' Research Service, July 2017.

[16] Zakem et al., 2017, p. 6; Zoran Arbutina, "Balkan Countries See Rise in Hate Speech," *Deutsche Welle*, February 24, 2017.

[17] "IRI's Center for Insights Poll: Crises in Europe and EU Leave Serbs Turning Toward Russia," International Republican Institute, December 2016; Pew Research Center, *Religious Belief and National Belonging in Central and Eastern Europe*, Washington, D.C., May 10, 2017, pp. 35–37; Rick Lyman, "Bulgaria Grows Uneasy as Trump Complicates Its Ties to Russia," *New York Times*, February 4, 2017.

[18] Radin and Reach, 2017, specifically Figure 2.1, p. 11.

Consequently, Russia aims to prevent any further encroachment of Western multilateral organizations, but their expansion into this region is not seen as an existential threat unless it is tied to particular initiatives, such as missile defense.[19] Russia might also view the region, which includes many of the newest and most vulnerable members of NATO and the EU, as an opportunity for undermining Western consensus by exposing the weaknesses of these new members and testing the West's ability to support them.

Finally, Western and Central European states are the least vulnerable to Russian gray zone tactics and are outside Russia's desired sphere of influence. These states are characterized by strong government institutions, relatively low corruption, general prosperity, and strong and independent media. Nevertheless, Moscow undertakes everyday gray zone actions throughout this region, because although they have the worst odds of succeeding, they also offer the highest potential payoff should they weaken a long-standing NATO or EU member's commitment to European unity. By dividing these organizations, Russia could also undermine the economic sanctions put in place against it after its invasion of Ukraine. Moreover, there are fissures in many Western and Central European states that Russia could potentially exploit—most notably, the immigration crisis, widespread dissatisfaction with the EU, and concerns about terrorism. Moscow has also curried favor with several populist and right-wing parties that promote nationalist, anti-integration agendas, such as Le Pen's National Rally in France.[20]

---

[19] The Balkan Regional Approach to Air Defense is a joint NATO and Balkan initiative, initiated in 2010, to provide air defense capabilities to the Balkans. It is intended to be integrated into the broader NATO ballistic missile defense system, which is viewed with suspicion by Russia. NATO Communications and Information Agency, *Balkan Regional Approach to Air Defence (BRAAD)*, Brussels: North Atlantic Treaty Organization, undated.

[20] David Chazan, "Russia 'Bought' Marine Le Pen's Support over Crimea," *The Telegraph*, April 4, 2015.

CHAPTER SEVEN

Civilian Organizations, Rather Than the Military, Might Be Best Positioned to Counter Most Russian Gray Zone Tactics

NATO and its member states' armed forces have focused considerable attention on countering Russian gray zone actions. Clearly, there is an important role for the military in deterring high-order aggression, whether it is attempted through purely gray zone tactics or through conventional means—which almost surely will be coupled with gray zone activities—but the vast majority of Russian gray zone activities are not geared toward territorial gains, but instead are everyday operations seeking to enhance Russia's influence through nonmilitary means. In short, our research suggests that the fight against gray zone activities is primarily a social, political, and economic fight—not a military one. Our games illuminated this observation. Many of the Blue and Green teams in our games argued that this fight is better waged by civilian agencies and NGOs, whose core competencies lie in these domains. These players observed that the most effective countermeasures available to the Blue and Green teams were not military actions, but rather actions taken by the U.S. Department of State, ministries of foreign affairs or economy, or the United States Agency for International Development to strengthen governments and liberal institutions. These players viewed the military's role in countering Russian gray zone tactics as a supporting one, buttressing and reinforcing civilian activities, and something that needed to be included in a whole-of-government approach.

Moreover, the West should not simply react to Russian gray zone actions or try directly to counter them. Rather, the United States and Europe need to develop long-term strategies to address the underlying weaknesses in states that Russia's gray zone tactics try to exploit and build more resilient democratic societies that will be able to fend off these actions on their own.[1] This should include efforts to raise awareness about false news, strengthen independent journalism, improve media literacy, fight corruption, bolster the rule of law, and diversify Europe's energy sources to reduce Moscow's economic leverage, especially on less prosperous countries.

The military plays an important but limited role in countering Russian gray zone activities by improving cyber defenses, enhancing intelligence and counterintelligence capabilities, and building partner special forces capacity so that allies can independently and effectively respond to any Russian covert infiltrations. Additionally, to improve responsiveness, the United States should encourage collaboration between law enforcement and the military, so that intelligence can be shared in a timely fashion and to ensure that a country has clearly delineated the roles and responsibilities of different government organizations in the event that Russia employs violent gray zone tactics.[2] In general, however, security force assistance, especially targeting general-purpose forces, should be a lower priority than efforts to strengthen civilian government institutions, the media, and civil society when seeking to counter gray zone tactics. NATO and its member states' armed forces should remain focused on bolstering conventional and nuclear deterrence while enhancing crisis stability, not on Russia's gray zone tactics.

---

[1]   Mazarr, 2015, pp. 118, 126.

[2]   We thank Dara Massicot for this point.

CHAPTER EIGHT

The West Might Be Winning This Competition, but Does Not Recognize It

Although many question whether Russia would ever overtly attack the Baltics or any NATO member, few disagree with the contention that Russia takes gray zone actions against nations in Europe and the United States on a daily basis.[1] These everyday Russian gray zone operations have caused concern verging on the point of panic and defeatism in some parts of Washington and Brussels.[2] These sentiments seem mostly to stem from the idea that the West cannot stop Russia from using gray zone activities; therefore, it is somehow *losing*. These sentiments—echoed by many players in our games—neglect an evaluation of the larger strategic situation. Our games provided important insights on this point.

Generally, players agreed that it is very difficult to decisively prove what effect everyday gray zone tactics have had in a myriad of countries. At this time, the only conclusion we can reach is that Russia has been actively interfering in electoral contests; there is no conclusive

---

[1]   Michael Kofman, "Fixing NATO Deterrence in the East Or: How I Stopped Worrying and Love NATO's Crushing Defeat by Russia," *War on the Rocks,* May 12, 2016.

[2]   Daniel R. Coats, "Statement for the Record: Worldwide Threat Assessment of the U.S. Intelligence Community," Office of the Director of National Intelligence, February 13, 2018; European Union External Action Service, *Joint Communication: Increasing Resilience and Bolstering Capabilities to Address Hybrid Threats*, Brussels: European External Action Service, June 13, 2018; "Countering 'Hybrid' Security Threats a Priority, Says EU," *EUbusiness,* July 19, 2017; Frank Jordans, "European Spy Chiefs Warn of Hybrid Threats from Russia, IS," Associated Press, May 14, 2018; Julian E. Barnes, "'Warning Lights Are Blinking Red,' Top Intelligence Officer Says of Russian Attacks," *New York Times,* July 13, 2018.

evidence, however, that those efforts affected the outcomes.[3] After the French public was alerted to the fact that Russia was backing Le Pen, Moscow's gray zone tactics might have even backfired, contributing to a decisive victory for Emmanuel Macron.

By stepping back and taking a wider look at the situation, it appears that the West might *not* be losing. Russian gray zone tactics are now the normal state of affairs.[4] After one game, a player observed that the West cannot force Russia to desist in these actions, but it is far from clear that they are having much effect. Russia's largest victories— in Crimea and the perhaps Pyrrhic victory in the Donbass—have combined gray zone techniques with more traditional applications of military power, but these outcomes are the exception—not the norm.[5] Moreover, in the Donbass, gray zone tactics alone did not bring victory, and now Moscow is bogged down in an increasingly costly war against a determined Ukrainian resistance. At the same time, the Russian economy is in the midst of an economic crisis exacerbated by the international sanctions put in place after its offensives in Ukraine. More significantly, Russia's offensives in Crimea and the Donbass have unified and galvanized Europe in a way that was unimaginable only four years ago. In that short time span, NATO has gone from shrinking and consolidating its military posture to expanding it, pushing forces farther eastward in an effort to bolster the defenses of the Baltic states. As one of the Blue players observed, Russia's gray zone aggression in Crimea and conventional offensive in eastern Ukraine have succeeded in preventing Ukraine from entering the EU, but have reignited a strategic competition with the West, which Russia is not winning and, in the long term, cannot win.[6]

---

[3]   U.S. Senate, 2018, p. 2; Indictment, *United States of America v. Internet Research Agency,* Case 1:18-cr-00032-DLF (D.D.C. Feb. 16, 2018); Indictment, *United States of America v. Viktor Borisovich Netyksho,* Case 1:18-cr-00215-ABJ (D.D.C. July 13, 2018).

[4]   Mazarr, 2015, p. 107, warns of a sense of "relentless confrontation" or "persistent warfare."

[5]   Mazarr, 2015, p. 121.

[6]   Russia has several key weaknesses, most notably its economy, its demographic issues, and its authoritarian kleptocratic regime. Joss Meakins, "Why Russia Is Far Less Threatening Than It Seems," *Washington Post,* March 8, 2017. For a contrary perspective which argues

Just because Moscow has not gained a significant advantage with its gray zone activities to date does not mean that the West should ignore these Russian actions. The United States and its European allies need to take steps to strengthen their defenses against gray zone tactics and to improve their ability to identify when Russia is shifting from everyday gray zone tactics to a more targeted campaign. Even the strongest states need to combat "truth decay"—which Russian gray zone tactics contribute to—by expanding awareness about disinformation and teaching how to distinguish facts from fiction.[7] Additionally, they should shore up defenses by addressing critical cyber vulnerabilities. These steps will not entirely stamp out Russian gray zone actions, but by addressing critical vulnerabilities, they will increase the ability of a society to withstand them. The EU and NATO also need to work to strengthen the resiliency of weaker states by building democratic, civilian institutions and an independent media, both of which are the most vulnerable targets of gray zone aggression.[8]

In short, just because the West might be ahead in this competition does not mean that it can ignore gray zone aggression. At the same time, however, the United States and its European allies should not overreact. Russia's greatest tactical successes largely depended on its conventional military forces, not the gray zone tools that supplemented them.[9] High-order aggression is something that can be stopped through conventional deterrence. If Washington and Brussels focus most of their efforts on stopping Russian social media trolls, countering each false news story, and promoting their own strategic narrative,

---

that Russia's strategy of raiding could succeed, see Michael Kofman, "Raiding and International Brigandry: Russia's Strategy for Great Power Competition," *War on the Rocks*, June 14, 2018.

[7]   Jennifer Kavanagh and Michael D. Rich, *Truth Decay: An Initial Exploration of the Diminishing Role of Facts and Analysis in American Public Life*, Santa Monica, Calif.: RAND Corporation, RR-2314-RC, 2018.

[8]   Brittany Beaulieu and David Salvo, "NATO and Asymmetric Threats: A Blueprint for Defense and Deterrence," *GMF Alliance for Security Democracy*, Policy Brief, No. 031, 2018, p. 5.

[9]   For more on Russia's conventional military, see Scott Boston and Dara Massicot, *The Russian Way of Warfare: A Primer*, Santa Monica, Calif.: RAND Corporation, PE-231-A, 2017.

Russian gray zone activities could turn into a cost-imposing strategy that distracts the West from the main competition. If NATO wants to deter Russian aggression, whether it uses gray zone tactics or not, it should put in place sufficient military capabilities to stop Russia from quickly achieving its objectives when the gray zone threatens to turn red.

Russia's gray zone tactics will persist and should be countered by hardening Western societies against Russian propaganda and its disinformation and attempts to undermine democracy. However, overreaction only serves Moscow's purposes. Strong civil societies and robust democratic institutions, not panic at "losing" or attempts to fight Russia blow-by-blow, are the West's best defenses against Russia's gray zone tactics. Russia's gray zone tactics signify its weakness, and the West's stronger political, cultural, and social systems will prevail over them if given the chance.

Wargaming the Gray Zone

The research documented in this report is drawn from a series of war games developed and conducted to explore a gray zone competition in Europe. These games were held between October 2016 and December 2017 and played by SMEs in Europe, Russia, and the United States.

Three distinct strategic political-military games were designed to conduct this research. The first game was a loosely structured argument-based matrix game and the next two games were card-driven games that differed in structure. All three games allowed players to take actions across different domains, with an emphasis on information, economic, military, and political-social actions. The scope of these games was varied as well, with the first two games allowing for free play within Europe and the last game limited to the Western Balkans. This final game built on the previous two games and incorporated insights derived from the earlier exercises to develop a tightly scoped and structured strategic level card-driven game.

The loose structure and seminar-style nature of the matrix game proved to be ill-suited to representing the nature of a gray zone competition, but helped us to identify key issues that merited further exploration. Because the variety of possible gray zone activities seemed limitless, the players were overwhelmed by the choices. Without a gaming platform to bound and focus the discussion, the players tended to fixate on covert tactical actions instead of the strategic competition. We initially attempted to provide more structure through simply adding cards that served as a menu for Blue, Red, and Green actions, but this proved disappointing as well, because it did not provide the players with the appropriate level of strategic feedback about the outcomes of their decisions. Free play within all of Europe further compounded the problem because unconstrained geography impeded the players' efforts to develop a strategy and resulted in a deluge of unconnected actions that inundated the adjudicators and interfered with learning.

Ultimately, we developed a three-sided card-driven board game focused on Russian, American, and European gray zone actions in the Western Balkans. At first blush, our gray zone game looks similar to commercial games, such as Twilight Struggle.[1] The game consists of two game boards (seen in Figures A.1 and A.2)—a game timeline where players made their short- and long-term actions by laying down their cards, and the other illustrating the state of play in the Balkans, including key country-level information and larger metrics of success, including NATO unity and Russian regime stability.

Cards provide a starting menu of actions that the Russia, Europe, and U.S. teams could play overtly or covertly (i.e., playing the card face-down) on the game timeline board. In spite of this structure, the gray zone game was also constructed to maximize its flexibility so that the players could amend the provided cards, create new cards, and develop their own narrative by expanding on the cards and overtly messaging to partners and adversaries alike. Adjudication of these actions used a simple model that reflected our best understanding of how and why gray zone tactics succeed or fail. To inform the development of this model, we surveyed the empirical record on Russian gray zone tactics and the existing literature on the individual actions that are considered to be a part of gray zone activities (e.g., information warfare, covert action). Based on this literature and SME elicitation, we created combat results tables and probabilistically assigned outcomes to different gray zone tactics. The purpose of the structured adjudication, however, was not to predict what could or will happen in the real world. Rather, it is to focus the discussion and to allow for the systematic exploration of Red gray zone actions and Blue and Green countermeasures. Moreover, with the exception of covert actions, adjudication was done transparently, so the players could understand the outcomes and argue with the control team if the adjudication seemed off. If the white cell, or game adjudicators, were persuaded by these arguments, they would amend the rules in real time.

---

[1]   Ananda Gupta and Jason Matthews, *Twilight Struggle*, GMT Games, 2015.

Figure A.1
Gray Zone Timeline Board

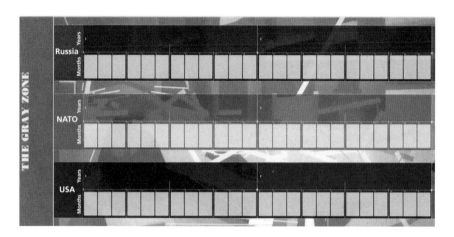

Figure A.2
Main Gray Zone Game Board

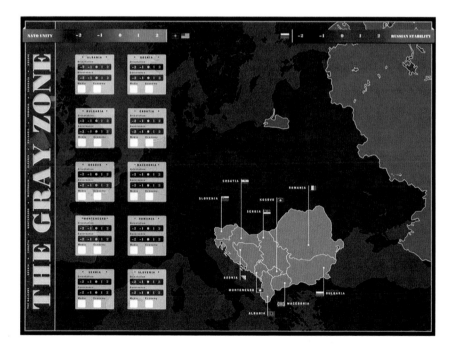

References

Adamsky, Dmitry, *Cross-Domain Coercion: The Current Russian Art of Strategy*, Proliferation Papers, No. 54, IFRI Security Studies Center, November 2015. As of July 30, 2018:
https://www.ifri.org/sites/default/files/atoms/files/pp54adamsky.pdf

Arbutina, Zoran, "Balkan Countries See Rise in Hate Speech," *Deutsche Welle*, February 24, 2017. As of July 25, 2018:
http://www.dw.com/en/balkan-countries-see-rise-in-hate-speech/a-37711134

Asymmetric Operations Working Group, *Ambiguous Threats and External Influences in the Baltic States, Phase 2: Assessing the Threat*, Ft. Meade, Md.: U.S. Army Asymmetric Warfare Group, Johns Hopkins Applied Physics Laboratory, November 2015.

Baker, Mark, "Drinking Games," *Foreign Policy*, July 29, 2015. As of July 31, 2018:
https://foreignpolicy.com/2015/07/29/
drinking-games-moldova-russia-eu-wine-embargo/

Barnes, Julian E., "'Warning Lights Are Blinking Red,' Top Intelligence Officer Says of Russian Attacks," *New York Times*, July 13, 2018. As of July 31, 2018:
https://www.nytimes.com/2018/07/13/us/politics/dan-coats-intelligence-russia-cyber-warning.html

Barno, David, and Nora Bensahel, "Fighting and Winning in the 'Gray Zone,'" *War on the Rocks,* May 19, 2015. As of July 25, 2018:
https://warontherocks.com/2015/05/fighting-and-winning-in-the-gray-zone/

Beaulieu, Brittany, and David Salvo, "NATO and Asymmetric Threats: A Blueprint for Defense and Deterrence," GMF Alliance for Securing Democracy, Policy Brief, No. 031, 2018. As of July 31, 2018:
https://securingdemocracy.gmfus.org/wp-content/uploads/2018/07/NATO-and-Asymmetric-Threats.pdf

Belford, Audrey, Saska Cvetkovska, Biljana Sekulovska, and Stevan Dojçinovic, "Leaked Documents Show Russian, Serbian Attempts to Meddle in Macedonia," OCCRP, Spooks and Spin in the Balkans, blog post, June 4, 2017.

Bergmann, Max, and Carolyn Kenney, *War by Other Means*, Washington, D.C.: Center for American Progress, June 6, 2017. As of July 25, 2018:
https://www.americanprogress.org/issues/security/reports/2017/06/06/433345/war-by-other-means/

Berzina, Ieva, "Russia's Compatriot Policy in the Nordic-Baltic Region," in *Russia's Footprint in the Nordic-Baltic Information Environment*, Report 2016/1027, Riga, Latvia: NATO Strategic Communications Centre of Excellence, January 2018, pp. 31–56.

Borger, Julian, "Russian-Trained Mercenaries Back Bosnia's Serb Separatists," *The Guardian*, January 12, 2018. As of July 25, 2018:
https://www.theguardian.com/world/2018/jan/12/russian-trained-mercenaries-back-bosnias-serb-separatists

Boston, Scott, and Dara Massicot, *The Russian Way of Warfare: A Primer*, Santa Monica, Calif.: RAND Corporation, PE-231-A, 2017. As of July 31, 2018:
https://www.rand.org/pubs/perspectives/PE231.html

Brands, Hal, "Paradoxes of the Gray Zone," Foreign Policy Research Institute, February 5, 2016. As of July 25, 2018:
https://www.fpri.org/article/2016/02/paradoxes-gray-zone

Burgess, Matt, "Here's the First Evidence Russia Used Twitter to Influence Brexit," *Wired*, November 10, 2017. As of July 25, 2018:
http://www.wired.co.uk/article/brexit-russia-influence-twitter-bots-internet-research-agency

Charap, Samuel, "The Ghost of Hybrid War," *Survival*, Vol. 57, No. 6, December 2015–January 2016, pp. 51–58.

Chazan, David, "Russia 'Bought' Marine Le Pen's Support over Crimea," *The Telegraph*, April 4, 2015. As of July 25, 2018:
https://www.telegraph.co.uk/news/worldnews/europe/france/11515835/Russia-bought-Marine-Le-Pens-support-over-Crimea.html

Chekinov, S. G., and S. A. Bogdanov, "Asimmetrichnyye mery po obespecheniyu voyennoy bezopasnosti Rossii [Asymmetrical Actions to Ensure Russia's Military Security]," *Voyennaya mysl' [Military Thought]*, No. 3, 2010, pp. 46–53.

Chivvis, Christopher S., *Understanding Russian 'Hybrid Warfare' and What Can Be Done About it Addendum*, testimony before the U.S. House of Representatives Armed Services Committee, Washington, D.C., March 22, 2017.

Coats, Daniel R., "Statement for the Record: Worldwide Threat Assessment of the U.S. Intelligence Community," Office of the Director of National Intelligence, February 13, 2018. As of July 31, 2018:
https://www.dni.gov/index.php/newsroom/congressional-testimonies/item/1845-statement-for-the-record-worldwide-threat-assessment-of-the-us-intelligence-community

Cohen, Ariel, and Robert E. Hamilton, *The Russian Military and the Georgia War: Lessons and Implications*, Carlisle, Pa.: Strategic Studies Institute, June 2011.

Cohen, Raphael S., and Andrew Radin, *Russia's Hostile Measures in Europe: Understanding the Threat*, Santa Monica, Calif.: RAND Corporation, RR-1793-A, 2019. As of October 2, 2019:
https://www.rand.org/pubs/research_reports/RR1793.html

Connell, Mary E., and Ryan Evans, *Russia's 'Ambiguous Warfare' and Implications for the U.S. Marine Corps*, Arlington, Va.: CNA, May 2015.

"Countering 'Hybrid' Security Threats a Priority, Says EU," *EUbusiness*, July 19, 2017. As of July 31, 2018:
https://www.eubusiness.com/news-eu/hybrid-threats.19xd/

Crosby, Alan, "Here Are the Flashpoints You Should Be Watching in the Balkans," Radio Free Europe/Radio Liberty, April 28, 2017. As of July 31, 2018:
https://www.rferl.org/a/balkans-flashpoint-to-watch-macedonia-serbia-kosovo-montenegro-bosnia/28456971.html

Curry, John, and Tim Price, *Matrix Games for Modern Wargaming: Developments in Professional and Educational Wargames Innovations in Wargaming*, Vol. 2, Barking, UK: Lulu Press, Inc., August 2014.

Davis, Joshua, "Hackers Take Down the Most Wired Country in Europe," *Wired*, August 21, 2007. As of July 25, 2018:
https://www.wired.com/2007/08/ff-estonia/

Devitt, Polina, "Russia Bans Polish Fruit and Vegetable in Apparent Retaliation for Sanctions," Reuters, July 30, 2014. As of July 31, 2018:
https://www.reuters.com/article/us-europe-russia-trade-poland/russia-bans-polish-fruit-and-vegetable-in-apparent-retaliation-for-sanctions-idUSKBN0FZ12220140730

Economist Intelligence Unit, "Russia's Role in the Western Balkans," webpage, October 18, 2017. As of July 31, 2018:
http://country.eiu.com/article.aspx?articleid=946003478&Country=Montenegro&topic=Politics&subtopic=Forecast&subsubtopic=International+relations

Elkus, Adam, "50 Shades of Gray: Why the Gray Wars Concept Lacks Strategic Sense," *War on the Rocks*, December 15, 2015. As of July 25, 2018:
https://warontherocks.com/2015/12/50-shades-of-gray-why-the-gray-wars-concept-lacks-strategic-sense/

European Union External Action Service, *Joint Communication: Increasing Resilience and Bolstering Capabilities to Address Hybrid Threats*, Brussels, June 13, 2018. As of July 31, 2018:
https://eeas.europa.eu/headquarters/headquarters-homepage/46397/joint-communication-increasing-resilience-and-bolstering-capabilities-address-hybrid-threats_en

Fund for Peace, "Fragile States Index," webpage, 2019. As of October 15, 2019:
https://fragilestatesindex.org/

Galeotti, Mark, "The 'Gerasimov Doctrine' and Russian Non-Linear War," *In Moscow's Shadow*, blog post, July 6, 2014. As of July 25, 2018:
https://inmoscowsshadows.wordpress.com/2014/07/06/
the-gerasimov-doctrine-and-russian-non-linear-war/

————, "Hybrid, Ambiguous, and Non-Linear? How New Is Russia's New Way of War?" *Small Wars and Insurgencies*, Vol. 27, No. 2, 2016, pp. 282–301. As of July 30, 2018:
https://www.tandfonline.com/doi/full/10.1080/09592318.2015.1129170

————, *Crimintern: How the Kremlin Uses Russia's Criminal Networks in Europe*, London: European Council on Foreign Relations, April 2017. As of July 31, 2018:
https://www.ecfr.eu/publications/summary/
crimintern_how_the_kremlin_uses_russias_criminal_networks_in_europe

————, "An Unusual Friendship: Bikers and the Kremlin," *Moscow Times*, May 19, 2015. As of July 31, 2018:
https://themoscowtimes.com/articles/
an-unusual-friendship-bikers-and-the-kremlin-op-ed-46671

Gerasimov, Valery, "Znacheniye nauki nakhoditsya v predvidenii: novyye vyzovy trebuyut pereosmysleniya form i metodov vedeniya boyevykh deystviy [The Value of Science Is in Foresight: New Challenges Demand Rethinking the Forms and Methods of Carrying Out Combat Operations]," *Voyenno-Promyshlennyy Kuryer [Military Courier]*, February 26, 2013.

Goltz, Thomas, "Letter from Eurasia: The Hidden Russian Hand," *Foreign Policy*, No. 92, Autumn 1993, pp. 92–116.

Greenberg, Andy, "The NSA Confirms It: Russia Hacked French Election 'Infrastructure,'" *Wired*, May 9, 2017. As of July 25, 2018:
https://www.wired.com/2017/05/
nsa-director-confirms-russia-hacked-french-election-infrastructure/

Greenslade, Roy, "Journalists Covering the Ukraine Crisis Suffer Intimidation," *The Guardian*, July 23, 2014. As of July 25, 2018:
https://www.theguardian.com/media/greenslade/2014/jul/23/
journalist-safety-ukraine

Grigas, Agnia, "How Soft Power Works: Russian Passportization and Compatriot Policies Paved Way for Crimean Annexation and War in Donbas," Atlantic Council, webpage, February 22, 2016. As of July 24, 2018:
http://www.atlanticcouncil.org/blogs/ukrainealert/how-soft-power-works-russian-passportization-and-compatriot-policies-paved-way-for-crimean-annexation-and-war-in-donbas

Groll, Elias, "A Brief History of Attempted Russian Assassinations by Poison," *Foreign Policy*, March 9, 2018. As of July 25, 2018:
https://foreignpolicy.com/2018/03/09/a-brief-history-of-attempted-russian-assassinations-by-poison/

Gupta, Ananda, and Jason Matthews, *Twilight Struggle*, GMT Games, 2015.

Harris, Kira, "Russia's Fifth Column: The Influence of the Night Wolves Motorcycle Club," *Studies in Conflict and Terrorism*, 2018.

Helmus, Todd C., Elizabeth Bodine-Baron, Andrew Radin, Madeline Magnuson, Joshua Mendelsohn, William Marcellino, Andriy Bega, and Zev Winkelman, *Russian Social Media Influence: Understanding Russian Propaganda in Eastern Europe*, Santa Monica, Calif.: RAND Corporation, RR-2237-OSD, 2018. As of July 25, 2018:
https://www.rand.org/pubs/research_reports/RR2237.html

Herszenhorn, David M., "Crimea Votes to Secede from Ukraine as Russian Troops Keep Watch," *New York Times*, March 16, 2014. As of July 31, 2018:
https://www.nytimes.com/2014/03/17/world/europe/crimea-ukraine-secession-vote-referendum.html

Higgins, Andrew, "Russian Money Suspected Behind Fracking Protests," *New York Times*, November 30, 2014. As of July 31, 2018:
https://www.nytimes.com/2014/12/01/world/russian-money-suspected-behind-fracking-protests.html

———, "In Expanding Russian Influence, Faith Combines with Firepower," *New York Times*, September 13, 2016a. As of July 24, 2018:
https://www.nytimes.com/2016/09/14/world/europe/russia-orthodox-church.html

———, "In Russia's 'Frozen Zone,' a Creeping Border with Georgia," *New York Times*, October 23, 2016b. As of July 31, 2018:
https://www.nytimes.com/2016/10/24/world/europe/in-russias-frozen-zone-a-creeping-border-with-georgia.html

———, "Russia's Feared 'Night Wolves' Bike Gang Came to Bosnia. Bosnia Giggled," *New York Times*, March 31, 2018. As of July 24, 2018:
https://www.nytimes.com/2018/03/31/world/europe/balkans-russia-night-wolves-republika-srpska-bosnia.html

Higgins, Andrew, Michael R. Gordon, and Andrew E. Kramer, "Photos Link Masked Men in East Ukraine to Russia," *New York Times*, April 20, 2014. As of July 25, 2018:
https://www.nytimes.com/2014/04/21/world/europe/photos-link-masked-men-in-east-ukraine-to-russia.html

Hoellerbauer, Simon, "Baltic Energy Sources: Diversifying Away from Russia," Foreign Policy Research Institute, June 14, 2017. As of July 25, 2018:
https://www.fpri.org/article/2017/06/baltic-energy-sources-diversifying-away-russia/

Hoffman, Frank, "On Not-So-New Warfare: Political Warfare vs Hybrid Threats," *War on the Rocks,* July 28, 2014. As of July 30, 2018:
https://warontherocks.com/2014/07/
on-not-so-new-warfare-political-warfare-vs-hybrid-threats/

———, "The Contemporary Spectrum of Conflict: Protracted, Gray Zone, Ambiguous, and Hybrid Modes of War," in Dakota L. Wood, ed., *2016 Index of Military Strength: Assessing America's Ability to Provide for the Common Defense,* Washington, D.C.: Heritage Foundation, 2015, pp. 25–36.

Holcomb, Franklin, *The Kremlin's Irregular Army: Ukrainian Separatist Order of Battle,* Russia and Ukraine Security Report 3, Washington, D.C.: Institute for the Study of War, September 2017. As of July 31, 2018:
http://www.understandingwar.org/backgrounder/
kremlin%E2%80%99s-irregular-army-ukrainian-separatist-order-battle

Holland, Emily, and Rebecca Friedman Lissner, "Countering Russian Influence in the Balkans," *Lawfare,* August 6, 2017. As of July 25, 2018:
https://www.lawfareblog.com/countering-russian-influence-balkans

Hope, Kerin, "Russia Meddles in Greek Town to Push Back the West," *Financial Times,* July 13, 2018. As of July 30, 2018:
https://www.ft.com/content/b5728090-86b0-11e8-96dd-fa565ec55929

"In U.N. Lawsuit, Ukraine Demands Russia End Support for Separatists," Reuters, January 17, 2017. As of July 24, 2018:
https://www.reuters.com/article/us-ukraine-crisis-russia-court-idUSKBN1511EU

Indictment, *United States of America v. Internet Research Agency,* Case 1:18-cr-00032-DLF (D.D.C. Feb. 16, 2018). As of July 31, 2018:
https://www.justice.gov/file/1035477/download

Indictment, *United States of America v. Viktor Borisovich Netyksho,* Case 1:18-cr-00215-ABJ (D.D.C. July 13, 2018). As of July 31, 2018:
https://www.justice.gov/file/1080281/download

"IRI's Center for Insights Poll: Crises in Europe and EU Leave Serbs Turning Toward Russia," International Republican Institute, December 2016. As of July 25, 2018:
http://www.iri.org/resource/iri%E2%80%99s-center-insights-poll-crises-europe-and-eu-leave-serbs-turning-toward-russia

Jackson, Van, "Tactics of Strategic Competition: Gray Zones, Redlines, and Conflicts Before War," *Naval War College Review,* Vol. 70, No. 3, Summer 2017, pp. 39–61.

Johnson, Keith, "Russia's Quiet War Against European Fracking," *Foreign Policy,* June 2014. As of July 31, 2018:
https://foreignpolicy.com/2014/06/20/russias-quiet-war-against-european-fracking/

Jolkina, Alexandra, and Markian Ostaptschuk, "Activists or Kremlin Agents—Who Protects Russian-Speakers in the Baltics?" *Deutsche Welle*, December 9, 2015. As of July 25, 2018:
https://www.dw.com/en/activists-or-kremlin-agents-who-protects-russian-speakers-in-the-baltics/a-18903695

Jones, Sam, "Estonia Ready to Deal with Russia's 'Little Green Men,'" *Financial Times*, May 13, 2015. As of July 31, 2018:
https://www.ft.com/content/03c5ebde-f95a-11e4-ae65-00144feab7de

Jones, Sam, Guy Chazan, and Christian Oliver, "NATO Claims Moscow Funding Anti-Fracking Groups," *Financial Times*, June 19, 2014. As of July 31, 2018:
https://www.ft.com/content/20201c36-f7db-11e3-baf5-00144feabdc0

Jordans, Frank, "European Spy Chiefs Warn of Hybrid Threats from Russia, IS," Associated Press, May 14, 2018. As of July 31, 2018:
https://apnews.com/65c1a2a9ca0d46ac9ff77efe38c8fbba

Joyce, Stephanie, "Along a Shifting Border, Georgia and Russia Maintain an Uneasy Peace," National Public Radio, March 13, 2017. As of July 24, 2018:
https://www.npr.org/sections/parallels/2017/03/13/519471110/along-a-shifting-border-georgia-and-russia-maintain-an-uneasy-peace

Kaljula, Diana, and Ivo Juurvee, "Narratives About the Nordic-Baltic Countries Promoted by Russia," in *Russia's Footprint in the Nordic-Baltic Information Environment*, Report 2016/1027, Riga, Latvia: NATO Strategic Communications Centre of Excellence, January 2018, pp. 57–78.

Kavanagh, Jennifer, and Michael D. Rich, *Truth Decay: An Initial Exploration of the Diminishing Role of Facts and Analysis in American Public Life*, Santa Monica, Calif.: RAND Corporation, RR-2314-RC, 2018. As of July 25, 2018:
https://www.rand.org/pubs/research_reports/RR2314.html

Kennan, George, "George F. Kennan on Organizing Political Warfare [Redacted Version]," Wilson Center Digital Archive, April 30, 1948. As of July 31, 2018:
https://digitalarchive.wilsoncenter.org/document/114320

Kofman, Michael, "Fixing NATO Deterrence in the East Or: How I Stopped Worrying and Love NATO's Crushing Defeat by Russia," *War on the Rocks,* May 12, 2016. As of July 25, 2018:
https://warontherocks.com/2016/05/fixing-nato-deterrence-in-the-east-or-how-i-learned-to-stop-worrying-and-love-natos-crushing-defeat-by-russia/

———, "Russian Hybrid Warfare and Other Dark Arts," *War on the Rocks*, March 11, 2016. As of July 25, 2018:
https://warontherocks.com/2016/03/russian-hybrid-warfare-and-other-dark-arts/

———, "Raiding and International Brigandry: Russia's Strategy for Great Power Competition," *War on the Rocks*, June 14, 2018. As of July 31, 2018:
https://warontherocks.com/2018/06/raiding-and-international-brigandry-russias-strategy-for-great-power-competition/

Kofman, Michael, Katya Migacheva, Brian Nichiporuk, Andrew Radin, Oleysa Tkacheva, and Jenny Oberholtzer, *Lessons from Russia's Operations in Crimea and Eastern Ukraine*, Santa Monica, Calif.: RAND Corporation, RR-1498-A, 2017. As of July 25, 2018:
https://www.rand.org/pubs/research_reports/RR1498.html

Kofman, Michael, and Matthew Rojansky, "A Closer Look at Russia's 'Hybrid War,'" *Kennan Cable,* No. 7, April 2015. As of July 25, 2018:
https://www.wilsoncenter.org/sites/default/files/7-KENNAN%20CABLE-ROJANSKY%20KOFMAN.pdf

Kogan, Rami, "Bedep Trojan Malware Spread by the Angler Exploit Kit Gets Political," *SpiderLabs Blog*, April 29, 2015. As of July 23, 2017:
https://www.trustwave.com/Resources/SpiderLabs-Blog/Bedep-trojan-malware-spread-by-the-Angler-exploit-kit-gets-political/

Kragh, Martin, and Sebastian Asberg, "Russia's Strategy for Influence Through Public Diplomacy and Active Measures: the Swedish Case," *Journal of Strategic Studies,* Vol. 40, No. 6, 2017, pp. 773–816.

Kucera, Joshua, "U.S. Intelligence: Russia Sabotaged BTC Pipeline Ahead of 2008 Georgia War," *EurasiaNet*, December 10, 2015. As of July 25, 2018:
https://eurasianet.org/us-intelligence-russia-sabotaged-btc-pipeline-ahead-of-2008-georgia-war

Lanoszka, Alexander, "Russian Hybrid Warfare and Extended Deterrence in Eastern Europe," *International Affairs*, Vol. 92, No. 1, 2016, pp. 175–195.

Lasheras, Francisco de Borja, Vessela Tcherneva, and Fredrik Wesslau, *Return to Instability: How Migration and Great Power Politics Threaten the Western Balkans,* London: European Council on Foreign Affairs, March 2016.

Lee, Dave, "The Tactics of a Russian Troll Farm," BBC News, February 16, 2018. As of July 25, 2018:
https://www.bbc.com/news/technology-43093390

"Libya, Migrants & Karma: Europe's New Migration Policy Wrecks on North African Reality," *RT,* July 22, 2018. As of July 30, 2018:
https://www.rt.com/news/433969-europe-refugee-crisis-migrants-libya/

Losh, Jack, "Putin's Angels: The Bikers Battling for Russia in Ukraine," *The Guardian*, January 29, 2016. As of July 31, 2018:
https://www.theguardian.com/world/2016/jan/29/russian-biker-gang-in-ukraine-night-wolves-putin

Lutonvinov, Vi, "I ispol'zovanie nevoennykh razvitie mer dlia ukrepleniia voennoi bezopasnosti Rossiiskoi Federatsii [The Use of Nonmilitary Development Measures to Strengthen the Military Security of the Russian Federation]," *Voennaia mysl' [Military Thought]*, No. 5, May 2009, pp. 2–12.

Lutsevych, Orysia, *Agents of the Russian World: Proxy Groups in the Contested Neighborhood*, London: Chatham House, Royal Institute of International Affairs, April 2016. As of July 31, 2018:
https://www.chathamhouse.org/publication/
agents-russian-world-proxy-groups-contested-neighbourhood

Lyman, Rick, "Bulgaria Grows Uneasy as Trump Complicates Its Ties to Russia," *New York Times*, February 4, 2017. As of July 25, 2018:
https://www.nytimes.com/2017/02/04/world/europe/
bulgaria-trump-russia-putin.html

MacDowall, Andrew, "Chevron's Bulgaria Pull-Out a Blow for Energy Security," *Financial Times,* June 11, 2014. As of July 31, 2018:
https://www.ft.com/content/347a30d3-d240-3a1b-9d7d-b07190dd90d3

Maigre, Merle, *Nothing New in Hybrid Warfare: The Estonian Experience and Recommendations for NATO*, German Marshall Fund of the United States, February 2015.

Mallonee, Laura, "Meet the People of a Soviet Country That Doesn't Exist," *Wired*, March 7, 2016. As of July 31, 2018:
https://www.wired.com/2016/03/
meet-people-transnistria-stuck-time-soviet-country-doesnt-exist/

Mazarr, Michael J., *Mastering the Gray Zone: Understanding a Changing Era of Conflict*, Carlisle, Pa.: Strategic Studies Institute and U.S. Army War College Press, December 2015.

McGuinness, Damien, "How a Cyber Attack Transformed Estonia," BBC News, April 27, 2017. As of July 25, 2018:
http://www.bbc.com/news/39655415

Meakins, Joss, "Why Russia Is Far Less Threatening Than It Seems," *Washington Post*, March 8, 2017. As of July 31, 2018:
https://www.washingtonpost.com/news/monkey-cage/wp/2017/03/08/
why-russia-is-far-less-threatening-than-it-seems/?utm_term=.9a6342e955b6

"Montenegro Begins Trial of Alleged Pro-Russian Coup Plotters," Reuters, July 19, 2017. As of July 24, 2018:
https://www.reuters.com/article/us-montenegro-election-trial/
montenegro-begins-trial-of-alleged-pro-russian-coup-plotters-idUSKBN1A413F

National Cyber Security Centre, UK Government Communications Headquarters, "Russian Military 'Almost Certainly' Responsible for Destructive 2017 Cyber-Attack," February 15, 2018. As of July 30, 2018:
https://www.ncsc.gov.uk/news/
russian-military-almost-certainly-responsible-destructive-2017-cyber-attack

NATO Communications and Information Agency, *Balkan Regional Approach to Air Defence (BRAAD)*, Brussels: North Atlantic Treaty Organization, undated. As of July 31, 2018:
https://www.ncia.nato.int/Documents/Agency%20publications/Balkan%20Regional%20Approach%20to%20Air%20Defence%20(BRAAD).pdf

Orttung, Robert, and Christopher Walker, "Putin's Frozen Conflicts," *Foreign Policy*, February 13, 2015. As of July 24, 2018:
https://foreignpolicy.com/2015/02/13/putins-frozen-conflicts/

Pallin, Caroline V., and Fredrik Westerlund, "Russia's War in Georgia: Lessons and Consequences," *Small Wars and Insurgencies*, Vol. 20, No. 2, 2009, pp. 400–424.

Paul, Christopher, and Miriam Matthews, *The Russian 'Firehose of Falsehood' Propaganda Model: Why It Might Work and Options to Counter It*, Santa Monica, Calif.: RAND Corporation, PE-198-OSD, 2016. As of July 25, 2018:
https://www.rand.org/pubs/perspectives/PE198.html

Petersen, Michael, "The Perils of Conventional Deterrence by Punishment," *War on the Rocks*, November 11, 2016. As of July 31, 2018:
https://warontherocks.com/2016/11/the-perils-of-conventional-deterrence-by-punishment/

Pew Research Center, *Religious Belief and National Belonging in Central and Eastern Europe,* May 10, 2017. As of July 25, 2018:
http://www.pewforum.org/2017/05/10/religious-belief-and-national-belonging-in-central-and-eastern-europe/

Polyakova, Alina, and Spencer Phipps Boyer, *The Future of Political Warfare: Russia, the West, and the Coming Age of Global Digital Competition*, Washington, D.C.: Brookings Institution, March 2018. As of July 30, 2018:
https://www.brookings.edu/research/the-future-of-political-warfare-russia-the-west-and-the-coming-age-of-global-digital-competition/

Racz, Andras, *Russia's Hybrid War in Ukraine: Breaking the Enemy's Ability to Resist*, FIIA Report 43, Helsinki, Finland: Finnish Institute of International Affairs, 2015.

Radin, Andrew, *Hybrid Warfare in the Baltics: Threats and Potential Responses*, Santa Monica, Calif.: RAND Corporation, RR-1577-AF, 2017. As of July 25, 2018:
https://www.rand.org/pubs/research_reports/RR1577.html

Radin, Andrew, and Clint Reach, *Russian Views of the International Order*, Santa Monica, Calif.: RAND Corporation, RR-1826-OSD, 2017. As of July 25, 2018:
https://www.rand.org/pubs/research_reports/RR1826.html

Romerstein, Herbert, "Disinformation as a KGB Weapon in the Cold War," *Journal of Intelligence History*, Vol. 1, No. 1, 2001, pp. 54–67.

Rosner, Thomas, "The Western Balkans: A Region of Secessions," *Deutsche Welle*, October 4, 2017. As of July 31, 2018:
https://www.dw.com/en/the-western-balkans-a-region-of-secessions/a-40793126

Roth, Andrew, "A Separatist Militia in Ukraine with Russian Fighters Holds a Key," *New York Times*, June 4, 2014a. As of July 31, 2018:
https://www.nytimes.com/2014/06/05/world/europe/in-ukraine-separatist-militia-with-russian-fighters-holds-a-key.html

———, "From Russia, 'Tourists' Stir the Protests," *New York Times,* March 3, 2014b. As of July 25, 2018:
https://www.nytimes.com/2014/03/04/world/europe/russias-hand-can-be-seen-in-the-protests.html

Russell, Martin, *At a Glance: Russia in the Western Balkans*, European Parliament Members' Research Service, July 2017. As of July 31, 2018:
http://www.europarl.europa.eu/thinktank/en/document.html?reference=EPRS_ATA%282017%29608627

"Russia's Sberbank to Get 40 Pct of Croatia's Agrokor After Debt Conversion," Reuters, June 8, 2018. As of July 24, 2018:
https://www.reuters.com/article/croatia-agrokor-sberbank/russias-sberbank-to-get-40-pct-of-croatias-agrokor-after-debt-conversion-idUSR4N1T800E

Russkiy Mir Foundation, "Russian Centers of the Russkiy Mir Foundation," webpage, undated. As of October 15, 2019:
https://russkiymir.ru/en/rucenter/

Schadlow, Nadia, "The Problem with Hybrid Warfare," *War on the Rocks,* April 2, 2015. As of July 28, 2015:
https://warontherocks.com/2015/04/the-problem-with-hybrid-warfare/

Scharre, Paul, "American Strategy and the Six Phases of Grief," *War on the Rocks,* October 6, 2016. As of July 25, 2018:
https://warontherocks.com/2016/10/american-strategy-and-the-six-phases-of-grief/

Schelling, Thomas C., *Arms and Influence*, New Haven, Conn.: Harvard University Press, 1966.

Schoen, Fletcher, and Christopher Lamb, *Deception, Disinformation, and Strategic Communications: How One Interagency Group Made a Major Difference*, Washington, D.C.: Institute for National Strategic Studies, June 2012.

Seddon, Max, and Michael Stothard, "Putin Awaits Return on Le Pen Investment," *Financial Times*, May 4, 2017. As of July 31, 2018:
https://www.ft.com/content/010eec62-30b5-11e7-9555-23ef563ecf9a

Shlapak, David A., *The Russia Challenge*, Santa Monica, Calif.: RAND Corporation, PE-250-A, 2018. As of July 31, 2018:
https://www.rand.org/pubs/perspectives/PE250.html

Shlapak, David A., and Michael W. Johnson, *Reinforcing Deterrence on NATO's Eastern Flank: Wargaming the Defense of the Baltics*, Santa Monica, Calif.: RAND Corporation, RR-1253-A, 2016. As of July 25, 2018:
https://www.rand.org/pubs/research_reports/RR1253.html

Shuster, Simon, "How Russian Voters Fueled the Rise of Germany's Far-Right," *Time*, September 25, 2017. As of July 30, 2018:
http://time.com/4955503/germany-elections-2017-far-right-russia-angela-merkel/

Singer, Peter W., "What We Didn't Learn from Twitter's News Dump on Russiagate," *Defense One*, January 20, 2018. As of July 25, 2018:
http://www.defenseone.com/ideas/2018/01/
twitter-and-russiagate-takeaways-friday-news-dump/145342/

Spruds, Andris, Anda Rozukaine, Klavs Sedlenieks, Martins Daugulis, Diana Potjomkina, Beatrix Tolgyesi, and Ilvija Brug, *Internet Trolling as a Tool of Hybrid Warfare: The Case of Latvia*, Riga, Latvia: NATO Strategic Communications Centre of Excellence, July 2015.

Szwed, Robert, *Framing of the Ukraine-Russia Conflict in Online and Social Media*, Riga, Latvia: NATO Strategic Communications Centre of Excellence, January 2018.

Tabor, Damon, "Putin's Angels: Inside Russia's Most Infamous Motorcycle Club," *Rolling Stone*, October 8, 2015. As of July 31, 2018:
https://www.rollingstone.com/culture/culture-news/
putins-angels-inside-russias-most-infamous-motorcycle-club-56360/

Trenin, Dmitri V., *Post Imperium: A Eurasian Story*, Washington, D.C.: Carnegie Endowment for International Peace, 2011.

Treverton, Gregory F., Andrew Thvedt, Alicia R. Chen, Kathy Lee, and Madeline McCue, *Addressing Hybrid Threats,* Stockholm: Swedish Defence University, European Center of Excellence for Countering Hybrid Threats, May 9, 2018. As of July 30, 2018:
https://www.hybridcoe.fi/wp-content/uploads/2018/05/Treverton-AddressingHybridThreats.pdf

U.S. Senate, *Disinformation: A Primer in Russian Active Measures and Influence Campaigns, Panel II: Hearing Before the Select Committee on Intelligence of the United States Senate*, Washington, D.C.: U.S. Government Publishing Office, March 30, 2017.

———, *Putin's Asymmetric Assault on Democracy in Russia and Europe: Implications for U.S. National Security*, minority staff report, Committee on Foreign Relations, Washington, D.C.: U.S. Government Publishing Office, January 10, 2018.

U.S. Special Operations Command, *The Gray Zone*, September 9, 2015.

"UPDATE 3-Russia Raises Gas Prices for Ukraine by 80 Percent," Reuters, April 3, 2014. As of July 24, 2018:
https://www.reuters.com/article/ukraine-crisis-gas-idUSL5N0MV2WL20140403

Ven Bruusgaard, Kristen, "Crimea and Russia's Strategic Overhaul," *Parameters*, Vol. 44, No. 3, Autumn 2014, pp. 81–90.

Von Der Burchard, Hans, "EU Takes Billion-Euro Battle to Russia," *Politico,* January 10, 2018. As of July 31, 2018:
https://www.politico.eu/article/
russia-sanctions-europe-trade-eu-takes-billion-euro-battle/

Votel, Joseph L., "Statement of General Joseph L. Votel, U.S. Army Commander, United States Special Operations Command Before the House Armed Services Committee Subcommittee on Emerging Threats and Capabilities," March 18, 2015. As of July 25, 2018:
http://docs.house.gov/meetings/AS/AS26/20150318/103157/HMTG-114-AS26-Wstate-VotelUSAJ-20150318.pdf

Vukicevic, Jasna, and Robert Coalson, "Russia's Friends Form New 'Cossak Army' in Balkans," Radio Free Europe/Radio Liberty, October 18, 2016. As of July 30, 2018:
https://www.rferl.org/a/balkans-russias-friends-form-new-cossack-army/
28061110.html

Wasser, Becca, Jenny Oberholtzer, Stacie L. Pettyjohn, and William Mackenzie, *Gaming the Gray Zone: Observations from Designing a Structured Gray Zone Strategy Game*, Santa Monica, Calif.: RAND Corporation, RR-2915-A, 2019. As of November 14, 2019:
https://www.rand.org/pubs/research_reports/RR2915.html

Watson, Ivan, and Sebastian Shukla, "Russian Fighter Jets 'Buzz' US Warship in Black Sea, Photos Show," CNN, February 16, 2017. As of July 24, 2018:
https://www.cnn.com/2017/02/16/us/russia-us-ship-fly-by/index.html

Wiggins, Warren, *War Game Adjudication: Adjudication Styles*, Newport, R.I.: United States Naval War College, 2014.

Willsher, Kim, and Jon Henley, "Emmanuel Macron's Campaign Hacked on Eve of French Election," *The Guardian*, May 6, 2017. As of July 25, 2018:
https://www.theguardian.com/world/2017/may/06/
emmanuel-macron-targeted-by-hackers-on-eve-of-french-election

World Bank Group, "Worldwide Governance Indicators," webpage, 2019. As of October 15, 2019:
https://info.worldbank.org/governance/wgi/#home

Zakem, Vera, Bill Rosenau, and Danielle Johnson, *Shining a Light on the Western Balkans: Internal Vulnerabilities and Malign Influence from Russia, Terrorism, and Transnational Organized Crime*, Arlington, Va.: CNA, May 2017.

Zakem, Vera, Paul Saunders, Umida Hashimova, and P. Kathleen Hammerberg, *Mapping Russian Media Network: Media's Role in Russian Foreign Policy and Decision-Making*, Arlington, Va.: CNA, January 2018.

Zgut, Edit, "Hungary's Pro-Kremlin Far Right Is a Regional Security Threat," *EU Observer*, December 23, 2016. As of July 30, 2018:
https://euobserver.com/opinion/136354